'Digging for China'

A Collection of Poetry

SELECTED AND ARRANGED BY
John O'Leary

Scholarstown Educational Publishers Ltd. London

Introduction

This is primarily a children's book. The selection has been loosely arranged into seasons so that the first quarter of the book has a broad autumnal theme, the second a broad winter theme and so on — but many poems encountered throughout do not, however, fit easily into any category.

John O'Leary

Illustrations by Mary Murphy.

ISBN 1 85276 031 1

Printed by Folens Publishing Co. Dublin 24

Contents

page

Digging *Edward Thomas* 7
From a Railway Carriage *Robert Louis Stevenson* 8
Requiem for the Croppies *Seamus Heaney* 9
My Sister Jane *Ted Hughes* 10
The Kwackagee *James Reeves* 11
The Listeners *Walter de la Mare* 12
Gruesome *Roger McGough* 14
The Bat *Theodore Roethke* 15
Legend *Judith Wright* 16
Interruption to a Journey *Norman MacCaig* 18
Sir Smasham Uppe *E. V. Rieu* 19
The Rescue *Hal Summers* 20
The Ballad of Father Gilligan *W. B. Yeats* 22
Piano Practice *Ian Serraillier* 24
The Old Pilot's Death *Donald Hall* 25

'Grave Undertones' 26-27

November *Thomas Hood* 28
The Witches' Spell *William Shakespeare* 29
The Shell *James Stephens* 30
Johnny *Emma Rounds* 31
The Old Woman of the Roads *Padraic Colum* 32
Coal Fire *Louis Untermeyer* 34
Miss Torrent *Ogden Nash* 35
The March to Kinsale *Aubrey De Vere* 36
The Boy who Laughed at Santa Claus *Ogden Nash* 38
Stopping by Woods on a Snowy Evening *Robert Frost* 41
The Computer's First Christmas Card *Edwin Morgan* 42
Death of a Snowman *Vernon Scannell* 43
The Father's Song (Translation from 'The Book of the Eskimoes') *Peter Freuchen* 44
Gertrude Conk *Spike Milligan* 45

'Sick Bay' 46-47

The Fight of the Year *Roger McGough* 48
London Spring, 1941 *Eiluned Lewis* 49
Mid-Term Break *Seamus Heaney* 50
Chivvy *Michael Rosen* 52
Danny Murphy *James Stephens* 53
Night Train to Istanbul *A. Elliott-Cannon* 54
A Removal from Terry Street *Douglas Dunn* 56
Hedgehog *Anthony Thwaite* 57
Clearing at Dawn *Li Po* 58
Two's Company *Raymond Wilson* 59
Tarantella *Hilaire Belloc* 60
Everybody Tells Me Everything *Ogden Nash* 61
The Nose *Ian Crichton Smith* 64
Bad Dog Brian Lee 62
Contrary Mary *Nancy Byrd Turner* 63
Morningtown (from 'Under Milk Wood') *Dylan Thomas* 65

Ogden Nash's Zoo 66

Summer Insects *Leonard Clark* 68
The Sea *James Reeves* 70
Helicopter *Gregory Harrison* 71
The Yellow Cat *Gregory Harrison* 72
Sneaky Bill *Willian Cole* 73
Colonel Fazackerley *Charles Causley* 74
Egg Thoughts *Russell Hoban* 75
The Alice Jean *Robert Graves* 76
The Meadow Mouse *Theodore Roethke* 78
The Starfish *Carmen Bernos De Gasztold* 80
'Running Lightly Over Spongy Ground' *Theodore Roethke* 82
John Barleycorn *Robert Burns* 84
Across the Pacific (from The Ballad of Kon Tiki) *Ian Serraillier* 86
Night Mail *W. H. Auden* 88
The Diver *Ian Serraillier* 90
Digging for China *Richard Wilbur* 91
The Snare *James Stephens* 92
The Wayfarer *Padraic Pearse* 93

The Limerick Train 94-95

Acknowledgements

The publishers wish to thank the following for permission to include copyright material in this collection:

"Digging for China" by Richard Wilbur from *Poems 1943-56,* by permission of Faber & Faber Ltd.; "The Starfish" from *The Beasts' Choir* by Carmen Bernos de Gasztold, translated by Rumer Godden, by permission of Macmillan, London, and Basingstoke; "Sir Smashum Uppe" by E.V. Rieu from *The Flattered Flying Fish,* by permission of Methuen and Co.; "A Removal from Terry Street" from *Terry Street* by Douglas Dunn, by permission of Faber and Faber Ltd.; "Interruption to a Journey" from *Selected Poems* by Norman MacCaig; "The Snare", "The Shell", "Danny Murphy" by James Stephens by permission of The Society of Authors on behalf of the copyright owner, Mrs. Iris Wise; "London Spring, 1941" by Eiluned Lewis by permission of The Society of Authors as the Literary Representative of the Estate of Eiluned Lewis; "Tarantella" from *Sonnets and Verse* by Hilaire Belloc, by permission of A.D. Peters & Co. Ltd.; "Mid-Term Break" and "Requiem for the Croppies" by Seamus Heaney from *Door Into The Dark* by permission of Faber & Faber Ltd.; "The Bat" and "The Meadow Mouse" by Theodore Roethke from *The Collected Poems of Theodore Roethke* by permission of Faber & Faber Ltd.; "Hedgehog" (from *Poems 1953-1983* by Anthony Thwaite, Secker & Warburg 1984), by permission of the author; "The Ballad of Anthony Thwaite, Secker & Warburg 1984), by permission of the author; "The Ballad of Father Gilligan" by W. B. Yeats from *The Collected Poems of W.B. Yeats,* by permission of A.P. Watt Ltd. on behalf of Michael B. Yeats and Macmillan London, Ltd.; "The Listeners" by Walter de la Mare, by permission of The Literary Trustees of Walter de la Mare and The Society of Authors as their representative; "Piano Practice," "The Diver" and "Across the Pacific" by Ian Serraillier, ©1952 and © 1963, by permission of the author; "Everybody Tells Me Everything", "The Camel", "The Kangaroo", "The Rhinoceros", "The Hippopotamos" from *Custard and Company* poems by Odgen Nash, selected by Quentin Blake (Kestrel Books, 1979), poems copyright © 1979 by the Estate of Odgen Nash, this selection copyright © 1979 by Quentin Blake, reproduced by permission of Penguin Books Ltd.; "Chivvy" by Michael Rosen from *You Tell Me,* poems by Roger McGough and Michael Rosen (Kestrel Books, 1979), p. 22, Michael Rosen poems copyright © 1979 by Michael Rosen, collection copyright © 1979 by Penguin Books Ltd.; "Bad Dog" from *Late Home* by Brian Lee (Kestrel Books, 1976), p. 11, copyright © 1976 by Brian Lee, reproduced by permission of Penguin Books Ltd.; "The Fight of the Year" by Roger McGough from *Watchwords* by permission of the author and Jonathan Cape Ltd.; "Stopping by Woods on a Snowy Evening" from *The Poetry of Robert Frost* edited by Edward Connery Lathem, by permission of the Estate of Robert Frost and Jonathan Cape Ltd.; "Legend" from *Selected Poems* by Judith Wright is reproduced by kind permission of Angus & Robertson (UK); "The Sea", "The Kwackagee" © James Reeves. Reprinted by permission of The James Reeves Estate,; "The Old Pilot's Death" by Donald Hall from the book *"A Roof of Tiger Lillies"* by kind permission of the author and André Deutsch Ltd.; "The Computer's First Christmas Card" by Edwin Morgan from the book *Poems of 30 Years* by kind permission of the author and Carcanet Press Ltd.; "Coal Fire" by Louis Untermeyer from *The Golden Treasury of Poetry* selected by Louis Untermeyer, published by Collins.

Suitable arrangements will be made with those holders of copyright whose permission had not been obtained at the time of going to press.

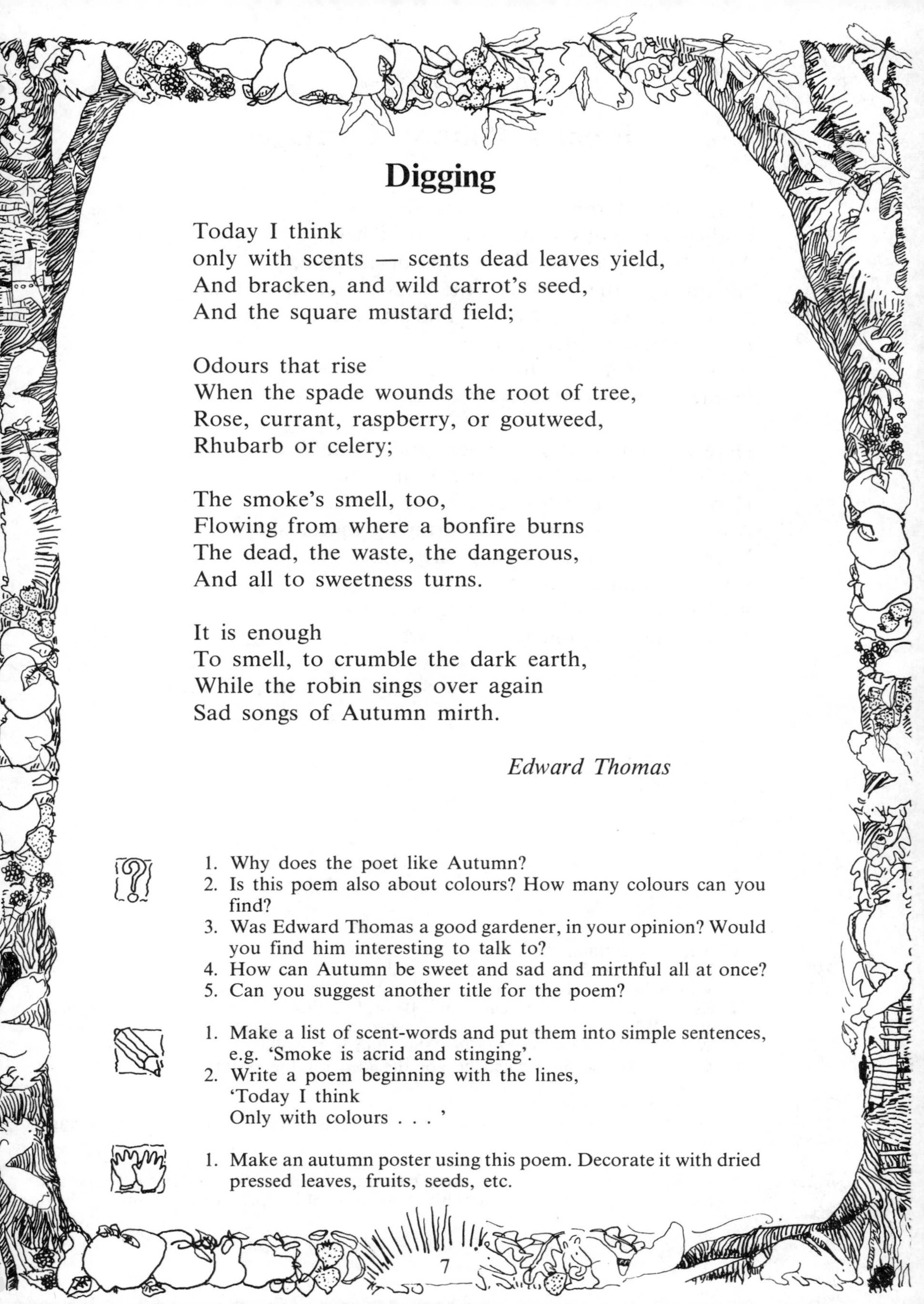

Digging

Today I think
only with scents — scents dead leaves yield,
And bracken, and wild carrot's seed,
And the square mustard field;

Odours that rise
When the spade wounds the root of tree,
Rose, currant, raspberry, or goutweed,
Rhubarb or celery;

The smoke's smell, too,
Flowing from where a bonfire burns
The dead, the waste, the dangerous,
And all to sweetness turns.

It is enough
To smell, to crumble the dark earth,
While the robin sings over again
Sad songs of Autumn mirth.

Edward Thomas

1. Why does the poet like Autumn?
2. Is this poem also about colours? How many colours can you find?
3. Was Edward Thomas a good gardener, in your opinion? Would you find him interesting to talk to?
4. How can Autumn be sweet and sad and mirthful all at once?
5. Can you suggest another title for the poem?

1. Make a list of scent-words and put them into simple sentences, e.g. 'Smoke is acrid and stinging'.
2. Write a poem beginning with the lines,
   'Today I think
   Only with colours . . . '

1. Make an autumn poster using this poem. Decorate it with dried pressed leaves, fruits, seeds, etc.

From a Railway Carriage

Faster than fairies, faster than witches,
Bridges and houses, hedges and ditches;
And charging along like troops in a battle,
All through the meadows the horses and cattle;
All of the sights of the hill and the plain
Fly as thick as driving rain;
And ever again, in the wink of an eye,
Painted stations whistle by.

Here is a child who clambers and scrambles,
All by himself and gathering brambles;
Here is a tramp who stands and gazes;
And there is the green for stringing the daisies!
Here is a cart run away in the road
Lumping along with man and load;
And here is a mill, and there is a river:
Each a glimpse and gone for ever!

R. L. Stevenson

1. Name everything the train passes.
2. Does the speed of the train ever change?
3. Which lines in the poem are noisy? Which lines are smooth?
4. Recite the last word in each line. Begin like this — "witches ditches, battle... etc.". What does a change in the word-sounds suggest?
5. Which phrases tell us how fast the train is travelling?
6. Where was the poet when he got the idea for the poem?

1. Write a movement poem to describe:
   (a) a horse running; (b) a person walking; (c) a marathon runner; (d) bouncing a ball.

1. Divide the class into two groups. One group will recite lines 1-4 in each verse and the second group lines 5-8. This is an enjoyable poem to learn off.

Requiem for the Croppies

The pockets of our great coats full of barley —
No kitchens on the run, no striking camp —
We moved quick and sudden in our own country.
The priest lay behind ditches with the tramp.
A people, hardly marching — on the hike —
We found new tactics happening each day:
We'd cut through reins and rider with the pike
And stampede cattle into infantry,
Then retreat through hedges where cavalry must be
thrown.
Until, on Vinegar Hill, the fatal conclave.
Terraced thousands died, shaking scythes at cannon.
The hillside blushed, soaked in our broken wave.
They buried us without shroud or coffin
And in August the barley grew up out of the grave,

Seamus Heaney

1. Who were the Croppies?
2. Is the speaker in the poem relaxed or frightened?
3. Are the speaker and his companions on the retreat or on the attack?
4. What do we know about their equipment and battle tactics?
5. Were they well-prepared to face the final battle on Vinegar Hill?
6. What does 'conclave' mean? Is this a suitable word to describe an army of ragged Croppies?
7. Explain 'the hillside blushed' in your own words.
8. What headstone marked the grave of the dead Croppies?
9. What is a requiem?

1. Imagine you are the speaker in the poem. Describe the action in diary form.

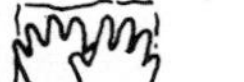

1. Paint a picture based on the poem.
2. The class might recite the poem and tape it. When it is played back it should sound like a prayer.
3. There are many ballads about the 1798 Rebellion. The class might sing or listen to such songs as 'The Croppy Boy' or 'Boolavogue'.
4. Play Beethoven: Symphony No. 7 in A, Second Movement. A taped sequence could be devised using poem, ballads and this sad piece of music.

My Sister Jane

And I say nothing — no, not a word
About our Jane. Haven't you heard
She's a bird, a bird, a bird, a bird.
Oh it never would do to let folks know
My sister's nothing but a great big crow.

Each day (we daren't send her to school)
She pulls on stockings of thick blue wool
To make her pin crow legs look right,
Then fits a wig of curls on tight,
And dark spectacles — a huge pair
To cover her very crowy stare.
Oh it never would do to let folks know
My sister's nothing but a great big crow.

When visitors come she sits upright
(With her wings and her tail tucked out of sight).
They think her queer but extremely polite.
Then when the visitors have gone
She whips out her wings and with her wig on
Whirls through the house at the height of your head —
Duck, duck, or she'll knock you dead.
Oh it never would do to let folks know
My sister's nothing but a great big crow.

At meals whatever she sees she'll stab it —
Because she's a crow and that's a crow habit.
My mother says, 'Jane! Your manners! Please!'
Then she'll sit quietly on the cheese,
Or play the piano nicely by dancing on the keys —
Oh it never would do to let folks know
My sister's nothing but a great big crow.

Ted Hughes

The Kwackagee

Back in the bleak and blurry days
When all was murk and mystery —
That is (if I may mint a phrase)
Before the dawn of history.
Professors think there used to be,
Not far from Waikee-waike,
A monster called the Kwackagee,
A sort of flying snake.

This animile, they all agree,
Was forty feet in length,
Would spiral up the tallest tree
And then with all his strength
Propel himself with sinuous grace
And undulation muscular
To find another feeding-place
In some far vale crepuscular.

Expert opinions are two
About his mode of travel,
Professor Grommit holds one view;
The other, Doctor Gravvle.
Grommit believes he could give off
Some kind of speed-emulsion;
The Doctor, ever prone to scoff,
Postulates jet-propulsion.

In prehistoric Waikee-waike,
The men (if men there were),
Would they in breathless terror quake
To hear that rattling whirr
As flew the monster through the sky?
Or would they brave the foe
With missile and with battle-cry?
The experts do not know.

James Reeves

The Listeners

'Is there anybody there?' said the Traveller,
  Knocking on the moonlit door;
And his horse in the silence champed the grasses
  Of the forest's ferny floor:
And a bird flew up out of the turret,
  Above the Traveller's head:
And he smote upon the door again a second time;
  'Is there anybody there?' he said,
But no one descended to the Traveller;
  No head from the leaf-fringed sill
Leaned over and looked into his gray eyes,
  Where he stood perplexed and still.
But only a host of phantom listeners
  That dwelt in the old house then
Stood listening in the quiet of the moonlight
  To that voice from the world of men:
Stood thronging the faint moonbeams on the dark stair,
  That goes down to the empty hall,
Hearkening in an air stirred and shaken
  By the lonely Traveller's call.'
And he felt in his heart their strangeness,
  Their stillness answering his cry,
While his horse moved, cropping the dark turf,
  'Neath the starred and leafy sky;
For he suddenly smote on the door, even
  Louder, and lifted his head: —
'Tell them I came, and no one answered,
  That I kept my word,' he said.
Never the least stir made the listeners,
  Though every word he spake
Fell echoing through the shadowiness of the still house
  From the one man left awake:
Ay, they heard the foot upon the stirrup,
  And the sound of iron on stone,
And how the silence surged softly backward
  When the plunging hoofs were gone.

Walter de la Mare

1. Which words and phrases tell us that the listeners were ghosts?
2. Describe the Traveller and his style of dress.
3. What were the Traveller's feelings as he stood in the moonlight?
4. What does 'the one man left awake' mean in your own words?
5. The Traveller said he had kept his word. What was his mission, do you think?
6. Find words similar in meaning to the following:
   champed, smote, perplexed, hearkening, thronging.
7. Find two words to describe how a person might feel when:
   (a) lonely; (b) happy; (c) frightened?
   e.g. uncertain — 'perplexed and still'.

1. Make up a conversation between the phantom listeners when the Traveller has gone.
2. You are the Traveller. You decide to break down the door.
   'The air was dry but bone-chilling. I saw on the staircase where the moonlight fell . . .'
   Continue the story.

1. Make up a mime and recitation based on the poem with five 'listeners' (miming), the Traveller, and the remainder of the class narrating.
2. Make a silhouette, based on the poem, of black figures on a grey background.

Gruesome

I was sitting in the sitting room
toying with some toys
when from a door marked: 'GRUESOME'
There came a GRUESOME noise.

Cautiously I opened it
and there to my surprise
a little GRUE lay sitting
with tears in its eyes

'Oh little GRUE please tell me
what is it ails thee so?'
'Well I'm so small,' he sobbed,
'GRUESSES don't want to know'

'Exercises are the answer,
Each morning you must DO SOME'
He thanked me, smiled,
and do you know what?
The very next day he...

Roger McGough

The Bat

By day the bat is cousin to the mouse.
He likes the attic of an ageing house.

His fingers make a hat about his head.
His pulse beat is so slow we think him dead.

He loops in crazy figures half the night
Among the trees that face the corner light.

But when he brushes up against a screen,
We are afraid of what our eyes have seen:

For something is amiss or out of place
When mice with wings can wear a human face.

Theodore Roethke

1. Can you explain why the bat would prefer an old house to a new one?
2. Describe a bat in your own words?
3. What do bats feed on? Why do they prefer darkness to daylight?
4. Why does the bat in the poem spend most of its time flitting near the corner light?
5. Are bats harmful? Could they possibly get entangled in your hair?
6. Do bats make nests? Do they lay eggs? How do they look after their babies?
7. Make up your own names for the bat. Here is one — 'flittermouse'.

1. You wake up suddenly one night. A huge bat is standing by your bed. He bows. He knows your name. He offers you a pair of goggles. 'Come fly with me . . .', says the bat. Continue.

1. Find out how many varieties of bats there are in Ireland. Find out their habits — what they eat, how they navigate, how they hibernate, etc.
2. Play some music from Strauss's 'Die Fledermaus'. Can you guess what 'fledermaus' means?

Legend

The blacksmith's boy went out with a rifle
and a black dog running behind.
Cobwebs snatched at his feet,
rivers hindered him,
thorn-branches caught at his eyes to make him blind
and the sky turned into an unlucky opal,
but he didn't mind,
I can break branches, I can swim rivers, I can stare out any
spider I meet,
said he to his dog and his rifle.

The blacksmith's boy went over the paddocks
with his old black hat on his head.
Mountains jumped in his way,
rocks rolled down on him,
and the old crow cried, 'You'll soon be dead.'
And the rain came down like mattocks.
But he only said
I can climb mountains, I can dodge rocks, I can shoot an old
crow any day,
And he went on over the paddocks.

When he came up to the end of the day the sun began falling.
Up came the night ready to swallow him,
like the barrel of a gun,
like an old black hat,
like a black dog hungry to follow him.
Then the pigeon, the magpie and the dove began wailing
and the grass lay down to pillow him.
His rifle broke, his hat blew away and his dog was gone
and the sun was falling.

But in front of the night the rainbow stood on the mountain,
just as his heart foretold.
He ran like a hare.
he climbed like a fox;
he caught it in his hands, the colours and the cold —
like a bar of ice, like the column of a fountain,
like a ring of gold.
The pigeon, the magpie and the dove flew up to stare,
and the grass stood up again on the mountain.

The blacksmith's boy hung the rainbow on his shoulder
instead of his broken gun.
Lizards ran out to see,
snakes made way for him,
and the rainbow shone as brightly as the sun.
All the world said, Nobody is braver, nobody is bolder,
nobody else has done
anything to equal it. He went home as bold as he could be
with the swinging rainbow on his shoulder.

Judith Wright

1. Name some of the difficulties the boy met as he set out?
2. Why is nature hindering him, do you think?
3. If you were the blacksmith's boy what things would frighten you?
4. Why does he decide to go on?
5. This boy has determination. Find two other words to describe him.
6. How will the mountains and the rivers treat him on his journey home?
7. Had the boy a reason for seeking out and taking the rainbow?
8. Is the poem describing one of the boy's daydreams?

1. The rainbow doesn't want to leave the mountain. How does the boy persuade it to go?
2. The rainbow has magical colouring powers. Make up an advertisement for the local paper stating some of the things the rainbow can do.

1. Draw a colourful picture of the boy returning home with the rainbow on his shoulder.

Interruption to a Journey

The hare we had run over
Bounced about the road
On the springing curve
Of its spine.

Cornfields breathed in the darkness,
We were going through the darkness and
The breathing cornfields from one
Important place to another.

We broke the hare's neck
And made that place, for a moment,
The most important place there was,
Where a bowstring was cut
And a bow broken forever
That had shot itself through so many
Darknesses and cornfields.

It was left in that landscape.
It left us in another.

Norman MacCaig

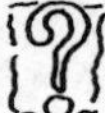

1. To what does the poet compare the cornfields?
2. Did this accident take place on the mountains or the lowlands?
3. What time of year was it?
4. Why does the poet compare the hare to a bowstring? Pick out a picture of the hare that resembles a bow.
5. How did the poet feel after the accident?
6. Could you compare the poet's journey to a bow? Explain.

1. Write a list of similes comparing the following animals to some object: (a) dog; (b) butterfly; (c) lion; (d) sleeping cat; (e) hamster
   e.g. 'A white mouse curled like a golf ball'

Sir Smasham Uppe

Good afternoon, Sir Smashum Uppe!
We're having tea: do take a cup!
Sugar and milk? Now let me see —
Two lumps, I think?... Good gracious me!
The silly thing slipped off your knee!
Pray don't apologise, old chap:
A very trivial mishap!
So clumsy of you? How absurd!
My dear Sir Smasham, not a word!
Now do sit down and have another,
And tell us all about your brother —
You know, the one who broke his head.
Is the poor fellow still in bed? —
A chair — allow me, sir!... Great Scott!
That *was* a nasty smash! Eh, what?
Oh, not at all: the chair was old —
Queen Anne, or so we have been told.
We've got at least a dozen more:
Just leave the pieces on the floor.
I want you to admire our view:
Come nearer to the window, do;
And look how beautiful... Tut, tut!
You didn't see that it was shut?
I hope you are not badly cut!
Not hurt? A fortunate escape!
Amazing! Not a single scrape!
And now, if you have finished tea,
I fancy you might like to see
A little thing or two I've got.
That china plate? Yes, worth a lot:
A beauty too... Ah, there it goes!
I trust it didn't hurt your toes?
Your elbow brushed it off the shelf?
Of course: I've done the same myself.
And now, my dear Sir Smasham — Oh,
You surely don't intend to go?
You *must* be off? Well, come again.
So glad you're fond of Porcelain.

E. V. Rieu

The Rescue

The boy climbed up into the tree.
The tree rocked. So did he.
He was trying to rescue a cat,
A cushion of a cat, from where it sat
In a high crutch of branches, mewing
As though to say to him, 'Nothing doing',
Whenever he shouted, 'Come on, come down.'
So up he climbed, and the whole town
Lay at his feet, round him the leaves
Fluttered like a lady's sleeves,
And the cat sat, and the wind blew so
That he would have flown had he let go.
At last he was high enough to scoop
That fat white cushion of nincompoop
And tuck her under his arm and turn
To go down — 
But oh! he began to learn
How high he was, how hard it would be,
Having come up with four limbs, to go down with three.
His heart-beats knocked as he tried to think:
He would put the cat in a lower chink —
She appealed to him with a cry of alarm
And put her eighteen claws in his arm.
So he stayed looking down for a minute or so,
To the good ground so far below.
When the minute began he saw it was hard;
When it ended he couldn't move a yard.
So there he was stuck, in the failing light
And the wind rising with the coming of the night.

His father! He shouted for all he was worth.
His father came nearer: 'What on earth — ?'
'I've got the cat up here but I'm stuck.'
'Hold on . . . ladder . . .', he heard. O luck!
How lovely behind the branches tossing
The globes at the pedestrian crossing
And the big fluorescent lamps glowed
Mauve-green on the main road.

But his father didn't come back, didn't come;
His little fingers were going numb.
The cat licked them as though to say
'Are you feeling cold? I'm O.K.'
He wanted to cry, he would count ten first,
But just as he was ready to burst
A torch came and his father and mother
And a ladder and the dog and his younger brother.
Up on a big branch stood his father,
His mother came to the top of the ladder,
His brother stood on a lower rung,
The dog sat still and put out its tongue.
From one to the other the cat was handed
And afterwards she was reprimanded.
After that it was easy, though the wind blew:
The parents came down, the boy came too
From the ladder, the lower branch and the upper
And all of them went indoors to supper,
And the tree rocked, and the moon sat
In the high branches like a white cat.

Hal Summers

1. Why do cats climb trees?
2. What lines in the poem tell us how windy the day was?
3. What would 'a cushion of a cat' look like?
4. Could the boy have rescued the cat in any other way?
5. How would you feel if you were trapped up in the tree with the cat?
6. 'What on earth — ', said the boy's father when he saw him up in the tree. What else did he say, do you think?
7. What could the boy see from his high perch?
8. Do you think his family were scared? Name the people who came out to watch the rescue?
9. What was the dog thinking as he looked up at the boy and the cat?
10. What is the meaning of 'reprimanded'?

1. Make up a conversation between the cat and the dog.
2. The boy's sister looks out her bedroom window later that night. She sees something in the branches of the tree. 'Help me, help me, please', cries the thing, 'I'm tangled'. It's a creature from the planet Aaargh. Tell the story.

Collect rescue stories from newspapers and magazines and pin them up in a special 'Rescue Unit' in your classroom. Stories can involve both people and animals.

The Ballad of Father Gilligan

The old priest Peter Gilligan
Was weary night and day;
For half his flock were in their beds,
Or under green sods lay.

Once, while he nodded on a chair,
At the moth-hour of eve,
Another poor man sent for him,
And he began to grieve.

'I have no rest, nor joy, nor peace,
For people die and die';
And after cried he, 'God forgive!
My body spake, not I!'

He knelt, and leaning on the chair
He prayed and fell asleep;
And the moth-hour went from the fields,
And stars began to peep.

They slowly into millions grew,
And leaves shook in the wind;
And God covered the world with shade,
And whispered to mankind.

Upon the time of sparrow-chirp
When the moths came once more,
The old priest Peter Gilligan
Stood upright on the floor.

'Mavrone, mavrone! the man has died
While I slept on the chair';
He roused his horse out of its sleep
And rode with little care.

He rode now as he never rode,
By rocky lane and fen;
The sick man's wife opened the door;
'Father! you come again!'

'And is the poor man dead?' he cried.
'He died an hour ago.'
The old priest Peter Gilligan
In grief swayed to and fro.

'When you were gone, he turned and died
As merry as a bird,'
The old priest Peter Gilligan
He knelt him at that word.

'He who hath made the night of stars
For souls who tire and bleed,
Sent one of His great angels down
To help me in my need.

'He who is wrapped in purple robes,
With planets in His care,
Had pity on the least of things
Asleep upon a chair.'

W.B. Yeats

1. How does Father Gilligan explain his own weariness?
2. When is the 'moth-hour of eve'?
3. How does the poet describe dawn?
4. Which words best describe Father Gilligan's feelings when he woke? — (a) surprised (b) guilty (c) frantic (d) irritated
5. Who listened to the dying man's Confession, in your opinion?
6. How did that incident change Father Gilligan's life?

1. Write your own one-line description of (a) dawn (b) noon (c) twilight (d) midnight.
2. You are Father Gilligan. You gallop to the sick man's house and find at the bedside — Father Gilligan! Continue the story.
3. Write a ballad about your favourite football star /TV hero/ friend.

1. Use the 'William Tell overture' by Mendelssohn in a taped sequence with the poem. You might play an excerpt after Verse 7.
2. Base a short play or mime on the poem. You could again use an excerpt from the 'William Tell Overture' to enliven the gallop sequence.

Piano Practice

A doting father once there was
Who loved his daughter Gerda,
Until she got the piano craze —
Then how the passion stirred her!
Her fingers were wild elephants' feet,
And as month after month he heard her.
He tried every way
To stop her play
From bribery to murder.

One day when she was practising,
He popped up behind and caught her
And dumped her in his wheelbarrow
And carried her off to slaughter.

Tipping her into a well, he cried,
'Hurrah! I've drowned my daughter!'
But a voice from the well
Rang out like a bell,
'Aha — there isn't any water!'

Ian Serraillier

The Old Pilot's Death

He discovers himself on an old airfield.
He thinks he was there before,
but rain has washed out the lettering of a sign.
A single biplane, all struts and wires,
stands in the long grass and wild flowers.
He pulls himself into the narrow cockpit
although his muscles are stiff
and sits like an egg in a nest of canvas.
He sees that the machine gun has rusted.
The glass over the instruments
has broken, and the red arrows are gone
from his gas gauge and his altimeter.
When he looks up, his propeller is turning.
although no one was there to snap it.
He lets out the throttle. The engine catches
and the propeller spins into the wind.
He bumps over holes in the grass,
and he remembers to pull back on the stick.
He rises from the land in a high bounce
which gets higher, and suddenly he is flying again.
He feels the old fear, and rising over the fields
the old gratitude. In the distance, circling
in a beam of late sun like birds migrating,
there are the wings of a thousand biplanes.
He banks and flies towards them.

Donald Hall

1. What is a biplane?
2. Is this a well-maintained aerodrome?
3. In which war would the plane have seen action?
4. What is an altimeter used for?
5. How do we know the pilot has flown from this aerodrome before?
6. Is the old pilot a ghost?
7. To where are the old pilot and his companions 'migrating'?

1. Write a story about the pilot's final battle?
2. You are the ghost of the old pilot. Your companions are flying above the aerodrome, waiting for you. The biplane refuses to start and you cannot join them. You are left alone. Tell what happens.

GRAVE UNDERTONES

Leslie Moore

Here lies what's left
Of Leslie Moore.
No Les
No more.

Ann Mann R.I.P.

Here lies the body of Ann Mann
Who lived an old woman
And died an old Mann.

Burton the Brewer

Here lies poor Burton,
He was both hale and stout;
Death laid him on his bitter bier,
Now in another world he hops about.

John Bun R.I.P.

Here lies John Bun;
He was killed by a gun.
His name was not Bun, but Wood;
But Wood would not rhyme with gun,
and Bun would.

Skugg R.I.P.

Here Skugg lies snug
As a bug in a rug.

Sir Vere-Burns R.I.P.

Here lies a man who was killed by lightning;
He died when his prospects seemed to be brightening.
He might have cut a flash in this world of trouble,
But the flash cut him, and he lies in the stubble.

A Dentist Lies Here

Stranger! Approach this spot with gravity!
John Brown is filling his last cavity.

Sir Isaac Letsome

When's people's ill they comes to I,
I physics, bleeds, and sweats 'em,
Sometimes they live, sometimes they die;
What's that to I? I Letsome.

Samuel Pease

Under this sod and beneath these trees
Lies all that's left of Samuel Pease.
Pease ain't here,
It's just his pod;
He shelled out his soul
Which flew to God.

Nell from Australia

God took our flower — our little Nell
He thought He too would like a smell.

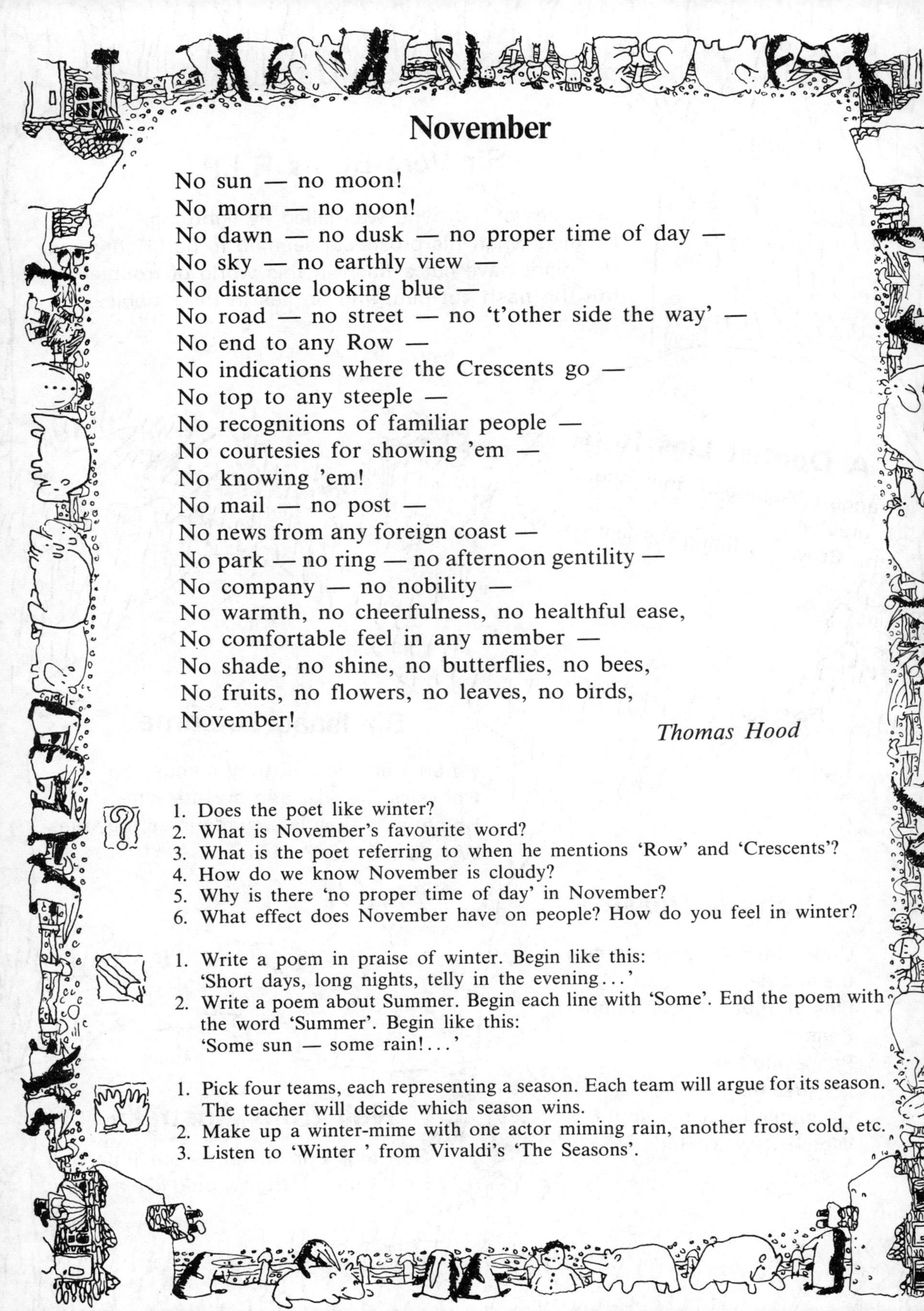

November

No sun — no moon!
No morn — no noon!
No dawn — no dusk — no proper time of day —
No sky — no earthly view —
No distance looking blue —
No road — no street — no 't'other side the way' —
No end to any Row —
No indications where the Crescents go —
No top to any steeple —
No recognitions of familiar people —
No courtesies for showing 'em —
No knowing 'em!
No mail — no post —
No news from any foreign coast —
No park — no ring — no afternoon gentility —
No company — no nobility —
No warmth, no cheerfulness, no healthful ease,
No comfortable feel in any member —
No shade, no shine, no butterflies, no bees,
No fruits, no flowers, no leaves, no birds,
November!

Thomas Hood

1. Does the poet like winter?
2. What is November's favourite word?
3. What is the poet referring to when he mentions 'Row' and 'Crescents'?
4. How do we know November is cloudy?
5. Why is there 'no proper time of day' in November?
6. What effect does November have on people? How do you feel in winter?

1. Write a poem in praise of winter. Begin like this:
   'Short days, long nights, telly in the evening...'
2. Write a poem about Summer. Begin each line with 'Some'. End the poem with the word 'Summer'. Begin like this:
   'Some sun — some rain!...'

1. Pick four teams, each representing a season. Each team will argue for its season. The teacher will decide which season wins.
2. Make up a winter-mime with one actor miming rain, another frost, cold, etc.
3. Listen to 'Winter ' from Vivaldi's 'The Seasons'.

The Witches' Spell

Double, double, toil and trouble;
Fire burn, and cauldron bubble.
Fillet of a fenny snake
In the cauldron boil and bake;
Eye of newt, and toe of frog,
Wool of bat, and tongue of dog,
Adder's fork, and blind-worm's sting,
Lizard's leg and owlet's wing,
For a charm of powerful trouble,
Like a hell-broth, boil and bubble.
Double, double, toil and trouble;
Fire burn, and cauldron bubble.

William Shakespeare

1. Why do witches make spells?
2. Do you know another word for cauldron?
3. How big is the cauldron in the poem, in your opinion?
4. Where are the witches?
5. List and draw the creatures mentioned in the poem.
6. Why did the witches include an 'adder's fork'? Do you know another word for 'fork'?
7. Tell what kind of 'powerful trouble' the spell will cause.

1. Make up your own spell using ingredients you might find in the kitchen. Begin like this:
   'Mouldy porridge, lumpy custard...
2. Write out a menu for Dracula's birthday party.

1. Act out this poem with three children playing the witches. The class can recite the two lines at the beginning and end.
2. Make a collage of the four witches around the cauldron.
3. You might listen to 'The Witch's Ride' from *Hansel and Gretel* by Humperdinck.

The Shell

And then I pressed the shell
Close to my ear
And listened well,
And straightway like a bell
Came low and clear
The slow, sad murmur of far distant seas,
Whipped by an icy breeze
Upon a shore
Wind-swept and desolate.
It was a sunless strand that never bore
The footprint of a man,
Nor felt the weight
Since time began
Of any human quality or stir
Save what the dreary winds and waves incur.
And in the hush of waters was the sound
Of pebbles rolling round.
For ever rolling with a hollow sound.
And bubbling sea-weeds as the waters go
Swish to and fro
Their long, cold tentacles of shiny grey.
There was no day,
Nor ever came a night
Setting the stars alight
To wonder at the moon;
Was twilight only and the frightened croon,
Smitten to whimpers, of the dreary wind
And waves that journeyed blind —
And then I loosed my ear — O, it was sweet
To hear a cart go jolting down the street.

James Stephens

1. What sounds do you hear when you place a shell to your ear?
2. How many 's' sounds can you count in line 6? What do those sounds remind you of?
3. Which words would you use to describe this strand?: (a) desolate; (b) beautiful; (c) sinister; (d) inviting.
4. Do you think tourists would find this place attractive?
5. You are a clever travel-agent. Write a brochure which makes the strand sound delightful. Include pictures.

1. Place your hands over your eyes and gaze into the sun or a very bright light. Write a poem about what you imagine.
   Begin like this:
   'I placed my hand over my eyes
   And straightaway I saw...'
2. Write a sentence to describe each of the following:
   (a) thunder;
   (b) a kettle boiling;
   (c) a television set after closedown;
   (d) cycling fast;
   (e) cold toothpaste;

1. Read 'Robinson Crusoe' by Daniel Defoe.
2. Collect pictures which show lonely or desolate scenes. Display them on the wall around a poster with the poem.

Johnny

Johnny used to find content
In standing always rather bent,
Like an inverted letter J.
His angry relatives would say,
'Stand up! don't slouch! You've got a spine,
Stand like a lamppost, not a vine!'
One day they heard an awful crack —
He'd stood up straight — it broke his back!

Emma Rounds

The Old Woman of the Roads

Oh, to have a little house!
To own the hearth and stool and all!
The heaped-up sods upon the fire,
The pile of turf against the wall!

To have a clock with weights and chains
And pendulum swinging up and down,
A dresser filled with shining delph,
Speckled and white and blue and brown!

I could be busy all the day
Clearing and sweeping the hearth and floor,
And fixing on their shelf again
My white and blue and speckled store!

I could be quiet there at night
Beside the fire and by myself,
Sure of a bed and loath to leave
The ticking clock and the shining delph!

Och! but I'm weary of mist and dark,
And roads where there's never a house nor bush,
And tired I am of bog and road.
And the crying wind and the lonesome hush!

And I am praying to God on high,
And I am praying him night and day,
For a little house, a house of my own —
Out of the wind's and the rain's way.

Padraic Colum

1. Give another title for this poem.
2. Is the house she describes old-fashioned or modern?
3. Make a list of the things the old woman would like to have in her house.
4. Make two columns. In one column make a list of sounds you might hear in the old woman's house. In the other column make a list of sounds you would hear in a modern house.
5. How does the old woman feel about life on the road?
6. Which words best describe the old woman?:
   (a) greedy; (b) weary; (c) easily-satisfied; (d) simple.

1. You are the old woman. It is 1986.
   You are wishing for a house. Begin like this:
   'Oh to have a little bungalow!
   To own the cooker, fridge and all! . .'
2. The old woman sees her dream-house advertised in a house-agent's window. Make up the advertisement. Include a picture.
3. The old woman gets her little house. One day a wolf appears on the doorstep, 'Good day', says the wolf, 'Are you little Red Riding Hood's granny?' Continue the story.

1. Organize a project on the houses of Ireland in times past. Make a list of facilities, house untensils etc. Make comparisons with modern lifestyles.

Coal Fire

And once, in some swamp-forest, these
Were trees.
Before the first fox thought to run,
These dead black chips were one
Green net to hold the sun.
Each leaf in turn was taught the right
Way to drink light;
The twigs were made to learn
How to catch flame and yet not burn;
Branch and then bough began to eat
Their diet of heat.
And so for years, six million years, or higher,
They held that fire.

And here, out of the splinters that remain,
The fire is loose again.
See how its hundred hands reach here and there,
Finger the air;
Then, growing bolder, twisting free,
It fastens on the remnants of the tree
And, one by one,
Consumes them; mounts beyond them; leaps; is done;
And goes back to the sun.

Louis Untermeyer

1. Why does the poet compare the leaves to 'one green net to hold the sun'?
2. The forest-top is a kind of school. Who are the pupils? What lessons are taught there?
3. Why is 'dead black chips' a good description of coal? Make up a description of your own.
4. What do the 'hundred hands' of a coal fire remind you of?
5. Give a brief description of a bonfire burning.
6. Make a list of words that describe fire and burning e.g. flickering

1. Collect information on fuels such as coal, oil, gas and how they are used, in homes, factories etc.
2. Paint a picture of the forest *but* all your trees must resemble people lifting their hands to the sun.

Miss Torrent

Little Miss Torrent drives a car.
Nothing surprising in that?
You'd think there was if you saw her ride by
Resplendent in flowery hat;
For little Miss Torrent,
Hunched over the wheel,
Scares everybody in town;
When people see her rushing along
They're sure she will batter them down.
They squirm as she crashes the gears and screams
With a stab of the brake to a stop;
They cover their faces to shut out the sight
As she spins on the ice like a top.
They daren't use the crossing
For fear she is blind
To the lollipop man with his stick;
As she squeezes the kerb with a squeal of her tyres
Pedestrians feel dizzy and sick.
But when you are driving yourself it is worst
For she scorches the old village street
As if she were driving a rallying car
With a champion racer to beat.
And by far worst of all are the deep narrow lanes
If you happen to see her approach,
For the lane is suddenly as dangerous as if
You were meeting a six-wheeler coach;
For she rarely pays heed to the motorist's code
And invariably drives the wrong side of the road.

Gregory Harrison

The March to Kinsale
(December 1601)

O'er many a river bridged with ice,
Through many a vale with snow-drifts dumb,
Past quaking fen and precipice
The Princes of the North are come!

Lo, these are they that year by year
Roll'd back the tide of England's war;—
Rejoice, Kinsale! thy help is near!
That wondrous winter march is o'er.

And thus they sang, 'Tomorrow morn
Our eyes shall rest upon the foe:
Roll on, swift night, in silence borne,
And blow, thou breeze of sunrise, blow!'

Blithe as a boy on marched the host,
With droning pipe and clear-voiced harp;
At last above that southern coast
Rang out their war-steeds' whinny sharp;
And up the sea-salt slopes they wound,
And airs once more of ocean quaff'd;
Those frosty woods the rocks that crown'd
As though May touched them, waved and laugh'd

And thus they sang, 'Tomorrow morn
Our eyes shall rest upon our foe:
Roll on, swift night, in silence borne,
And blow, thou breeze of sunrise, blow!'

Beside their watchfires couch'd all night
Some slept, some laugh'd, at cards some play'd,
While, chaunting on a central height
Of moonlit crag, the priesthood pray'd
And some to sweetheart, some to wife
Sent message kind; while others told
Triumphant tales of recent fight,
Or legends of their sires of old.

And thus they sang, 'Tomorrow morn
Our eyes at last shall see the foe:
Roll on, swift night, in silence borne,
And blow, thou breeze of sunrise, blow!'

Aubrey De Vere

1. Who were the 'Princes of the North'?
2. Was the march to Kinsale easy or difficult?
3. What instruments did the musicians play?
4. Give a brief description of this army on the move.
5. What does the song tell us about how the soldiers felt?
6. How did they spend the night before the battle?
7 What happened at the Battle of Kinsale?

1. You are one of O'Neill's officers. Record in diary-form the most difficult day you have experienced on the march to Kinsale.

1. On a map of Ireland trace the march of O'Neill and O'Donnell to Kinsale.
2. On the same map mark in the mountains, rivers etc. crossed by the army. Find out as much as you can about Kinsale.
3. Play the 'Redetsky March' by Johann Strauss Snr. and the march theme from Tchaikovsky's '1812 Overture'

The Boy who Laughed at Santa Claus

In Baltimore there lived a boy
He wasn't anybody's joy.
Although his name was Jabez Dawes,
His character was full of flaws.
In school he never led his classes,
He hid old ladies' reading glasses,
His mouth was open when he chewed,
And elbows to the table glued.

He stole the milk of hungry kittens,
And walked through doors marked
NO ADMITTANCE.
He said he acted thus because
There wasn't any Santa Claus.
Another trick that tickled Jabez
Was crying 'Boo!' at little babies.
He brushed his teeth, they said in town,
Sideways instead of up and down.

Yet people pardoned every sin,
And viewed his antics with a grin,
Till they were told by Jabez Dawes,
'There isn't any Santa Claus!'
Deploring how he did behave,
His parents swiftly sought their grave.
They hurried through the portals pearly,
And Jabez left the funeral early.

Like whooping cough, from child to child,
He sped to spread the rumour wild:
'Sure as my name is Jabez Dawes
There isn't any Santa Claus!'
Slunk like a weasel or a marten
Through nursery and kindergarten,
Whispering low to every tot,
'There isn't any, no there's not!'

The children wept all Christmas Eve
And Jabez chortled up his sleeve.
No infant dared hang up his stocking
For fear of Jabez' ribald mocking,
He sprawled on his untidy bed,
Fresh malice dancing in his head,
When presently with scalp a-tingling,
Jabez heard a distant jingling;
He heard the crunch of sleigh and hoof
Crisply alighting on the roof.

What good to rise and bar the door?
A shower of soot was on the floor.
What was beheld by Jabez Dawes?
The fireplace full of Santa Claus!
Then Jabez fell upon his knees
With cries of 'Don't,' and 'Pretty please'.
He howled, 'I don't know where you read it,
But anyhow, I never said it!'

'Jabez,' replied the angry saint,
'It isn't I, it's you that ain't.
Although there is a Santa Claus,
There isn't any Jabez Dawes!'
Said Jabez then with impudent vim,
'Oh, yes there is; and I am him!
Your magic don't scare me, it doesn't' —
And suddenly he found he wasn't!

From grimy feet to grimy locks,
Jabez became a Jack-in-the-box,
An ugly toy with springs unsprung,
Forever sticking out his tongue;
The neighbours heard his mournful squeal;
They searched for him, but not with zeal,
No trace was found of Jabez Dawes,
Which led to thunderous applause,
And people drank a loving cup
And went and hung their stockings up.

All you who sneer at Santa Claus,
Beware the fate of Jabez Dawes,
The saucy boy who mocked the saint.
Donder and Blitzen licked off his paint.

Ogden Nash

1. Which words best describe Jabez Dawes?:—
   (a) mischievous; (b) playful; (c) warm-hearted; (d) mean.
2. List three of the cruellest things he did.
3. What was Jabez Dawes' greatest crime?
4. Was Jabez a brave boy?
5. Was his punishment too severe?
6. Who were Donder and Blitzen?

1. You are the founder of the 'Be Kind To People Society'. Write out the 'Ten Rules of Kindness'.
2. Your aunt buys you a Jack-in-the-box for Christmas. You are disgusted. 'There isn't any Santa Claus', you whisper. Suddenly the Jack-in-the-box begins to change......
   Continue the story.

1. Form the 'Jabez Dawes Society' in your classroom. Each member must wear a Jack-in-the-box badge which you can make in the Art class. Make up your own rules!
2. Tape this poem. Jabez and Santa can be played by children. The sound effects should not be difficult.

Stopping by Woods on a Snowy Evening

Whose woods these are I think I know,
His house is in the village though;
He will not see me stopping here
To watch his woods fill up with snow.

My little horse must think it queer
To stop without a farmhouse near
Between the woods and frozen lake
The darkest evening of the year.

He gives his harness bells a shake
To ask if there is some mistake.
The only other sound's the sweep
Of easy wind and downy flake.

The woods are lovely, dark and deep,
But I have promises to keep,
And miles to go before I sleep,
And miles to go before I sleep.

Robert Frost

1. Why is the person in the poem afraid of being seen?
2. How does the little horse feel when they stop?
3. Imagine you are the person in the poem. Describe what you see around you.
4. Make two lists of words. In one list include the words in the poem that have 's' sounds. In the other include the words with 'ee' sounds.
5. Which description best suits the poem?:
   (a) colourful; (b) frightening; (c) quiet and mysterious.
6. Find a word similar in meaning to 'downy'.
7. Describe the sounds made by the horse and buggy as they travel along.
8. What promises must the poet keep, do you think?

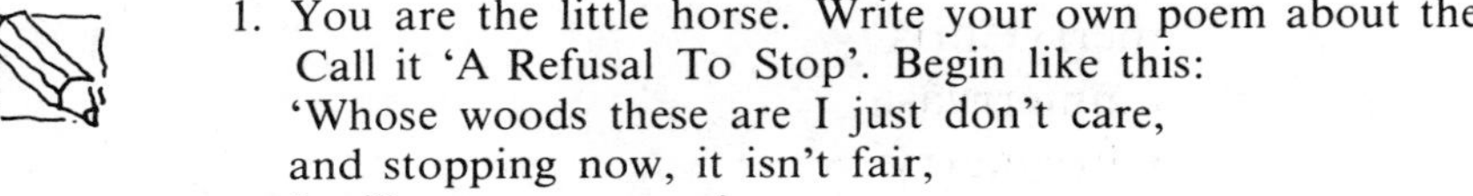

1. You are the little horse. Write your own poem about the incident.
   Call it 'A Refusal To Stop'. Begin like this:
   'Whose woods these are I just don't care,
   and stopping now, it isn't fair,
   I will not stop......'
2. You are the owner of the wood. You have been out hunting when suddenly you spot a buggy halted under the trees. You are filled with anger and fear. What is *your* secret?

1. Make a winter frieze showing the scenes described in the poem.

The Computer's First Christmas Card

jollymerry
hollyberry
jollyberry
merryholly
happyjolly
jollyjelly
jellybelly
bellymerry
hollyheppy
jollyMolly
marryJerry
merryHarry
hoppyBarry
heppyJarry
boppyheppy
berryjorry
jorryjolly
moppyjelly
Mollymerry
Jerryjolly
bellyboppy
jorryhoppy
hollymoppy
Barrymerry
Jarryhappy
happyboppy
boppyjolly
jollymerry
merrymerry
merrymerry
merryChris
ammerryasa
Chrismerry
asMERRYCHR
YSANTHEMUM

Edwin Morgan

Death of a Snowman

I was awake all night,
Big as a polar bear,
Strong and firm and white.
The tall black hat I wear
Was draped with ermine fur,
I felt so fit and well
Till the world began to stir
And the morning sun swell.
I was tired, began to yawn;
At noon in the humming sun
I caught a severe warm;
My nose began to run.
My hat grew black and fell.
Was followed by my great head.
There was no funeral bell,
But by tea-time I was dead.

Vernon Scannell

1. Who is speaking in the poem?
2. What is ermine?
3. How does the poem describe daybreak?
4. Why does the snowman say the sun was humming?
5. What did the sick snowman tell his doctor?
6. Do you think the snowman was suffering as he melted?

1. You discover a family of snow-imps living in the fridge. Explain how you save them when the electricity fails.
2. Make an Arctic list using the word 'snow', e.g. 'snow-water bottle', 'snowbathing'.
3. Write a poem called 'The Bored Snowman'. Begin with 'There's nothing to do in Antarctica...'

1. Organize a drama. One person can mime the melting snowman while the class recite the poem. Everybody can take a turn.
2. Make a life-size snowman in the classroom using sugar-paper and cotton wool.

The Father's Song

Great snowslide,
Stay away from my igloo,
I have my four children and my wife;
They can never enrich you.

Strong snowslide,
Roll past my weak house.
There sleep my dear ones in the world.
Snowslide, let their night be calm.

Sinister snowslide,
I just built an igloo here, sheltered from the wind.
It is my fault if it is put wrong.
Snowslide, hear me from your mountain.

Greedy snowslide,
There is enough to smash and smother.
Fall down over the ice;
Bury stones and cliffs and rocks.

Snowslide, I own so little in the world.
Keep away from my igloo, stop not our travels.
Nothing will you gain by our horror and death,
Mighty snowslide, mighty snowslide.

Little snowslide,
Four children and my wife are my whole world, all I own,
All I can lose, nothing can you gain.
Snowslide, save my house, stay on your summit.

Anonymous. Translated from the Eskimo by Peter Freuchan

1. What did the father mean when he told the snowslide that his wife and children could not 'enrich' it?
2. List all the requests the father makes of the snowslide.
3. Did the father build his igloo in a safe spot, in your opinion?
4. Where does he ask the snowslide to fall?
5. Which words best describe the father's feelings toward the snowslide?: (a) hatred (b) respect (c) fear (d) unconcern

1. Write a poem begging a shower of rain not to fall and spoil your game. Begin like this:
   'O, great wet, woolly-bellied waterbottle...'
2. Write the snowslide's reply to the father. Begin like this:
   'Little man
   In your tiny ice bubble...

1. Make a papier-mache model of the scene described in the poem. You might have the father peeping fearfully from the igloo.

Gertrude Conk

A rose is a rose is a rose,
And so is a nose is a nose.
Red is the rose,
So is the nose,
And that's how it goes, how it goes, how it goes...

A nose, I suppose, I suppose,
grows like a rose, like a rose.
Ah! but the rose
Unlike the *nose*
Doesn't honk! when it blows, when it blows, when it blows...

A nose, in the throes, in the throes
of a cold in der dose, in der dose.
Hip is a rose
Drip goes the nose,
And that's how it flows, how it flows, how it flows.

Spike Milligan

SICK BAY

Updated Hubbard

Old Mother Hubbard
Went to the cupboard
To get the poor dog a bone.
When she got there,
The cupboard was bare,
So the poor little doggie had Pal.

Spike Milligan

Two Sad

It's such a shock I almost screech,
When I find a worm inside my peach!
But then, what *really* makes me blue
Is to find a worm who's bit in two!

William Cole

Aunt Maud

I had written to Aunt Maud
Who was on a trip abroad,
When I heard she'd died of cramp
Just too late to save the stamp.

Anon.

The Canary

The song of Canaries
Never varies,
And when they're molting
They're pretty revolting.

Ogden Nash

Tenderheartedness

Bill, in one of his nice new sashes,
Fell in the fire and was burnt to ashes;
Now, although the room grows chilly,
I haven't the heart to poke poor Billy.

Harry Graham

The Stern Parent

Father heard his children scream,
So he threw them in the stream,
Saying, as he drowned the third,
Children should be seen not heard!'

Henry Graham

Little Willie

Little Willie from his mirror
Licked the mercury right off.
Thinking, in his childish error,
It would cure the whooping cough.

At the funeral his mother
Brightly said to Mrs Brown:
''Twas a chilly day for Willie
When the mercury went down!'

Anon.

Henry Sutton

Henry Sutton
Made his wife
Serve him mutton
All his life.

When going to sleep,
His mind was rested
By counting the sheep
That he'd digested!

Anon.

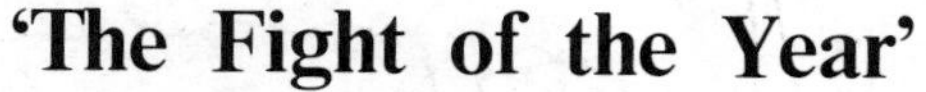

'The Fight of the Year'

'And there goes the bell for the third month
and Winter comes out of its corner looking groggy
Spring leads with a left to the head
followed by a sharp right to the body
    daffodils
    primroses
    crocuses
    snowdrops
    lilacs
    violets
    pussywillow
Winter can't take much more punishment
and Spring shows no sign of tiring
    tadpoles
    squirrels
    baalambs
    badgers
    bunny rabbits
    mad march hares
    horses and hounds
Spring is merciless
Winter won't go the full twelve rounds
    bobtail clouds
    scallywaggy winds
    the sun
    a pavement artist
    in every town
A left to the chin
and Winter's down!
    tomatoes
    radish
    cucumber
    onions
    beetroot
    celery
    and any
    amount
    of lettuce
    for dinner
Winter's out for the count
Spring is the winner!'

Roger Mc Gough

London Spring, 1941

If I could paint I'd show you
Something I saw to-day;
A house bombed, blasted sideways,
The roof blown clean away;
A bath perched near a chasm;
A waste of broken floors,
The staircase turned to matchwood
And twisted, tortured doors.
While in the neighbour's garden,
With slender fence and tree
Dividing all its modest length
From dark catastrophe,
A little Moses cradle
Was placed upon the ground
And in it slept a baby
So pink and sweet and round,
With no one there to mind it,
To fuss or fear, not one!
But all the jolly crocuses
Wide open to the sun.

Eiluned Lewis.

1. How many pictures of destruction can you find in the poem?
2. Apart from the baby, what else was unaffected by the bomb?
3. Which word, in particular, is used to describe the air-raids on London?
4. What is a Moses cradle? Where did it get its name? How can the baby be compared to Moses?
5. Which lines in the poem tell us that it is springtime?
6. Make up your own title for the poem

1. You are the pilot of the bomber. You are deeply saddened. Compose a prayer.
2. Write a poem to describe some event that stands out in your mind! Begin like this:
   'If I could paint I'd show you . .'

1. Draw or paint the scene described in the poem. Make sure that the crocuses are clearly seen in your picture.
2. Have a class debate. Should civilians have to suffer? Is the bombing of cities wrong? etc.
3. Make a tape using sound-effects to sound like an air-raid.

Mid-Term Break

I sat all morning in the college sick-bay
Counting bells knelling classes to a close.
At two o'clock our neighbours drove me home.

In the porch I met my father crying —
He had always taken funerals in his stride —
And Big Jim Evans saying it was a hard blow.

The baby cooed and laughed and rocked the pram
When I came in, and I was embarrassed
By old men standing up to shake my hand.

And tell me they were "sorry for my trouble".
Whispers informed strangers I was the eldest,
Away at school, as my mother held my hand

In hers and coughed out angry tearless sighs,
At ten o'clock the ambulance arrived
With the corpse, stanched and bandaged by the nurses.

Next morning I went up into the room. Snowdrops
And candles soothed the bedside; I saw him
For the first time in six weeks. Paler now,

Wearing a poppy bruise on his left temple,
He lay in the four foot box as in his cot.
No gaudy scars, the bumper knocked him clear.

A four foot box, a foot for every year.

Séamus Heaney

1. At what time of year did the tragedy occur?
2. What does 'knelling' mean? Do you think the poet used that word for a particular reason?
3. You are the boy. You have just been told of your little brother's death. Describe how you feel as you sit in the college sick-bay.
4. Why was he embarrassed when the old men shook his hand?
5. Why did his mother cough out 'angry tearless sighs'?
6. Do you find it unusual that the boy himself did not cry? Can you explain why?
7. Which words would best describe the boy's emotions?: (a) baffled; (b) disbelieving; (c) stunned; (d) confused.
8. Find other words for 'stanched', 'soothed', 'gaudy'.
9. How old was the boy's brother? How old was the boy, in your opinion?

1. Make up a conversation between the boy and his mother after the funeral.
2. Complete the following: e.g. 'His mother wept and raged'
   'His father...
   'Big Jim...
   'The boy...
3. List six particular occasions and the correct thing to say on each occasion, e.g. A death — 'I'm sorry for your trouble'.

Chivvy

Grown-ups say things like:
Speak up.
Don't talk with your mouth full
Don't stare
Don't point
Don't pick your nose
Sit up
Say please
Less noise
Shut the door behind you
Don't drag your feet
Haven't you got a hankie?

Take your hands out of your pockets
Pull your socks up
Stand up straight
Say thank you
Don't interrupt
No one thinks you're funny
Take your elbows off the table

Can't you make your *own*
mind up about anything?

Michael Rosen

Danny Murphy

He was as old as old could be.
His little eye could scarcely see,
His mouth was sunken in between
His nose and chin, and he was lean
And twisted up and withered quite,
So that he couldn't walk aright.

His pipe was always going out,
And then he'd have to search about
In all his pockets, and he'd mow —
O deary me! and, musha now!
And then he'd light his pipe, and then
He'd let it go clean out again.

He couldn't dance or jump or run,
Or ever have a bit of fun
Like me and Susan, when we shout
And jump and throw ourselves about —
But when he laughed, then you could see
He was as young as young could be!

James Stephens

1. How old was Danny Murphy, do you think?
2. How do you know he had no teeth?
3. Write a short description of Danny Murphy as a young man.
4. Write a short description of your best friend.
5. Find two words similar in meaning to 'mow'-
6. Would Danny Murphy have liked to jump about with the children?
7. Why does he appear 'as young as young can be' at the end of the poem?
8. Make a list of things old people say, e.g. 'Deary me... musha now'

1. If only the children had known Danny Murphy's terrible secret!
   You have found the 'Danny Murphy Files' in a dump. Wanted in ten countries for!!!... (Tell the story)

1. Make up a 'Wanted — £10,000 Reward' poster. Write a description of your mother/father/uncle etc. Include a picture.
2. Make up a little drama or mime about Oisin's return to Ireland.

Night Train to Istanbul

Some whispered tales which I have heard
Although I know they're quite absurd,
Say strange things happen on this train,
Things the Turks can't quite explain.
  Through the night to Istanbul,
  Roaring, rushing, through the night.

You lose your passport, or your life,
Your wallet and perhaps your wife;
Folks disappear, and blinds are drawn,
Before the border and the dawn.
  Through the night to Istanbul,
  Rocking, rolling, through the night.

Deals in diamonds, deadly drugs,
Lovely women, crooks, and thugs,
Coded plans and cold-eyed killers.
The kind of thing you meet in thrillers,
  Through the night to Istanbul,
  Rattling, raging, through the night.

I think that blonde might be a spy,
I cannot look her in the eye;
The slant-eyed man could be a crook;
The train attendant had that look.
  Through the night to Istanbul,
  Whistling, wailing, through the night.

I think they stretch a point or two,
I hardly think it can be true;
But if I'm killed I shall complain,
And never use this train again.
  Through the night to Istanbul,
  Rooting, tooting, through the night.

A. Elliott-Cannon

1. Where is Istanbul?
2. Is this a steam-train or a modern train?
3. What was the name of the famous express-train that used to travel between Paris and Istanbul?
4. Make a list of words to describe the train on its journey, e.g. 'hurtling'.
5. How would people 'disappear' on a train?
6. Make a passenger-list for this train. Include such notorious people as Count Vladimir Werewolf-Rambling and Princess Andrea Opensecret.
7. What is the poet's little joke in this poem?

1. You are on the Day-Train to Venice. Only the nicest people can hope to get tickets. Describe some of your fellow-passengers.
2. You are the chief poet of the tortoises. Compose a poem in praise of tortoise-travelling. Begin like this:

   'We like to travel at our ease
   We like to take our time..'

1. On a map of Europe plot out your own route between Paris and Istanbul. Make sure it takes you through the most important cities of Europe.
2. Paint a series of portraits of the people you have named in (6) above.

A Removal from Terry Street

On a squeaking cart, they push the usual stuff,
A mattress, bed ends, cups, carpets, chairs,
Four paperback westerns. Two whistling youths
In surplus U.S. Army battle-jackets
Remove their sister's goods. Her husband
Follows, carrying on his shoulders the son
Whose mischief we are glad to see removed,
And pushing, of all things, a lawnmower.
There is no grass in Terry Street. The worms
Come up cracks in concrete yards in moonlight.
That man, I wish him well. I wish him grass.

Douglas Dunn

1. Why are the people moving house, in your opinion?
2. Make a list of the things they are taking with them.
3. Why didn't they hire a furniture removal van, do you think?
4. Are the people of Terry Street wealthy?
5. Write an imaginary description of Terry Street.
6. What kind of mischief would the little boy have got up to?
7. Will the poet's wish for the owner of the lawnmower come true?
8. Read the last four lines and compose your own title for the poem.

1. You are a house-agent trying to sell a house in Terry Street. Make a poster to advertise it.
2. Your are a prisoner in an upstairs room in Terry Street. You have made friends with a carrier pigeon. You intend to send the pigeon to your teacher with instructions to rescue you. Include a careful description of Terry Street.

1. Make a collage-picture of Terry Street.
2. The painter L. S. Lowry painted many scenes like Terry Street. Ask your local librarian to help you find art-books that show the pictures of L. S. Lowry.

Hedgehog

Twitching the leaves just where the drainpipe clogs
In ivy leaves and mud, a purposeful
Creature at night about its business. Dogs
Fear his stiff seriousness. He chews away

At beetles, worms, slugs, frogs. Can kill a hen
With one snap of his jaws, can taunt a snake
To death on muscled spines. Old countrymen
Tell tales of hedgehogs sucking a cow dry.

But this one, cramped by houses, fences, walls,
Must have slept here all winter in that heap
Of compost, or have inched by intervals
Through tidy gardens to this ivy bed.

And here, dim-eyed, but ears so sensitive
A voice within the house can make him freeze,
He scuffs the edge of danger; yet can live
Happily in our nights and absences.

A country creature, wary, quiet and shrewd,
He takes the milk we give him, when we're gone.
At night, our slamming voices must seem crude
To one who sits and waits for silences.

Anthony Thwaite

Clearing at Dawn

The fields are chill, the sparse rain has stopped;
The colours of spring teem on every side.
With leaping fish the blue pond is full;
With singing thrushes the green boughs droop,
The flowers of the field have dabbled their powdered cheeks;
The mountain grasses are bent level at the waist.
By the bamboo stream the last fragment of cloud
Blown by the wind slowly scatters away.

Li Po

1. In which country is this poem set?
2. How many of the spring-scenes described might you also find in Ireland? List them.
3. To what are the flowers compared?
4. Which lines tell us that the weather is fine?
5. How many pictures of spring does the poem have?

1. Make up a picture-poem about the sounds of spring.
   Begin like this:
   'The sounds of spring come from every side.
   Rooks argue on trees, children on the road...'

Two's company

The sad story of the man who didn't believe in ghosts

They said the house was haunted, but
He laughed at them and said, 'Tut, tut!
I've never heard such tittle-tattle
As ghosts that groan and chains that rattle;
And just to prove I'm in the right,
Please leave me here to spend the night.'

They winked absurdly, tried to smother
Their ignorant laughter, nudged each other,
And left him just as dusk was falling
With a hunchback moon and screech-owls calling.
Not that this troubled him one bit;
In fact, he was quite glad of it,
Knowing it's every sane man's mission
To contradict all superstition.

But what is that? Outside it seemed
As if chains rattled, someone screamed!
Come, come, it's merely nerves, he's certain
(But just the same, he draws the curtain).
The stroke of twelve — but there's no clock!
He shuts the door and turns the lock
(Of course, he knows that no one's there.
But no harm's done by taking care!)
Someone's outside — the silly joker.
(He may as well pick up the poker!)
That noise again! He checks the doors,
Shutters the windows, makes a pause
To seek the safest place to hide —
(The cupboard's strong — he creeps inside).
'Not that there's anything to fear,'
He tells himself, when at his ear
A voice breathes softly, 'How do you do!
I am the ghost. Pray, who are you?

Raymond Wilson

Tarantella

Do you remember an Inn,
Miranda?
Do you remember an Inn?
And the tedding and the spreading
Of the straw for a bedding,
And the fleas that tease in the High Pyrenees,
And the wine that tasted of tar?
And the cheers and the jeers of the young muleteers
(Under the vine of the dark verandah)?
Do you remember an Inn, Miranda,
Do you remember an Inn?
And the cheers and the jeers of the young muleteers
Who hadn't got a penny,
And who weren't paying any
And the hammer at the doors and the Din?
And the Hip! Hop! Hap!
Of the clap
Of the hands to the twirl and the swirl
Of the girl gone chancing,
Glancing,
Dancing,
Backing and advancing,
Snapping of the clapper to the spin
Out and in —
And the Ting, Tong, Tang of the Guitar!
Do you remember an Inn,
Miranda?
Do you remember an Inn?
Never more;
Miranda,
Never more.
Only the high peaks hoar:
And Aragon a torrent at the door.
No sound
In the walls of the Halls where falls
The tread
Of the feet of the dead to the ground
No sound:
But the boom
Of the far Waterfall like Doom.

Hilaire Belloc

1. A tarantella is a kind of dance. Which words would best describe a tarantella? (a) rapid; (b) slow and graceful; (c) stiff; (d) whirling.
2. Read the poem and make two lists of dancing words. List all the short dancing words in one column and all the long dancing words in the other, e.g. 'twirl' and 'swirl' are short, 'glancing' and 'dancing' are long.
3. Name some of the musical instruments that might be used in playing a tarantella.
4. Which words, in your opinion, would best describe the feelings of the dancers?: (a) excited; (b) enchanted; (c) nervous; (d) bored.
5. Which words tell you that the dancers clap their hands?
6. Which lines tell you that the dancers are tired and out of breath?
7. Make a list of 'heavy words' that suggest the weariness of the dancers after the dance, e.g. 'falls', 'tread' . . .
8. Where are the Pyrenees? In what country is Aragon?

1. You are a hippopotamus. Write a poem about the 'Hippopotamella' which is the favourite dance of hippopotami. Begin like this:
   'Do you remember Africa,
   Molly?
   And our feet in the river muck . . .'

Everybody Tells Me Everything

I find it difficult to enthuse
Over the current news.
Just when you think that at least the outlook is so
black that it can grow no blacker, it worsens,
And that is why I do not like the news, because
there has never been an era when so many things
were going so right for so many of the wrong
persons.

Ogden Nash

Bad Dog

All day long, Bones hasn't been seen
— But now he comes slinking home
Smelling of ditches and streams
And pastures and pinewoods and loam
And tries to crawl under my bed.
His coat is caked with mud,
And one of his ears drips blood.
Nobody knows where he's been.

'Who did it?' they ask him, 'who...?
He'll have to be bathed... the sinner...
Pack him off to his basket...
You *bad dog,* you'll get no dinner...?
And he cowers, and rolls an eye.
Tomorrow, I *won't* let him go —
But he licks my hand, and then — oh,
How I wish that I had been too.

Brian Lee

1. Does the boy live in a town or in the country?
2. What has Bones been doing all day, do you think?
3. Why does Bones try to sneak in without being noticed?
4. Which words best describe the family's reaction?
   (a) anger (b) pity (c) disgust (d) concern
5. Write a description of Bones slinking into the house. Begin like this: — 'The door opened but at first nothing appeared. Then his head came cautiously around....'
6. Make a list of 'dog-words', e.g. 'slinking'
7. Describe the boy's feelings when Bones licks his hand?

1. It is early on the morning after. Bones is tugging at the boy's bedclothes. He wakes. 'I have found something incredible . . .' Bones whispers. You are the boy. Tell the story.
2. Make a list of gestures that people make. e.g. 'He rolled his eyes in disbelief'.
3. Write a poem about your pet dinosaur, Felix.

1. Bones is to be put on trial for continually upsetting the house. Mother is bringing the charges. The teacher can arrange a court-room scene in the class with children playing mother, father, boy, judge, witnesses etc.

Contrary Mary

You ask why Mary was called contrary?
Well, this is why, my dear;
She planted the most outlandish things
In her garden every year:
She was always sowing the queerest seed,
And when advised to stop,
Her answer was merely, 'No, indeed —
Just wait till you see the crop!'

And here are some of the crops, my child
(Although not nearly all);
Bananarcissus and cucumberries,
And violettuce small;
Potatomatoes, melonions rare,
And rhubarberries round,
With porcupineapples prickly-rough
On a little bush close to the ground.

She gathered the stuff in mid-July
And sent it away to sell —
And now you'll see how she earned her name,
And how she earned it well.
Were the crops hauled off in a farmer's cart?
No, not by any means,
But in little June-buggies and automobeetles
And dragonflying machines!

Nancy Byrd Turner

The Nose

(after Gogol)

The nose went away by itself
in the early morning
while its owner was asleep.
It walked along the road
sniffing at everything.

It thought: I have a personality of my own.
Why should I be attached to a body?
I haven't been allowed to flower.
So much of me has been wasted.

And it felt wholly free.
It almost began to dance
The world was so full of scents
it had had no time to notice,

when it was attached to a face
weeping, being blown, catching all sorts of
germs
and changing colour.

But now it was quite at ease
bowling merrily along
like a hoop or a wheel,
a factory packed with scent.

And all would have been well
but that, round about evening,
having no eyes for guides,
it staggered into the path
of a mouth, and it was gobbled
rapidly like a sausage
and chewed by great sour teeth —
and that was how it died.

Ian Crichton Smith

Morningtown
(From 'Under Milk Wood')

There's the clip clop of horses on the sunhoneyed cobbles of the humming streets, hammering of horse-shoes, gobble quack and cackle, tomtit twitter from the bird-ounced boughs, braying on Donkey Down. Bread is baking, pigs are grunting, chop goes the butcher, milk-churns bell, tills ring, sheep cough, dogs shout, saws sing. Oh, the Spring whinny and morning moo from the clog dancing farms, the gulls' gab and rabble on the boat-bobbing river and sea and the cockles bubbling in the sand, scamper of sander-lings, curlew cry, crow caw, pigeon coo, clock strike, bull bellow, and the ragged gabble of the beargarden school as the women scratch and babble in Mrs Organ Morgan's general shop where everything is sold: custard, buckets, henna, rat-traps, shrimp-nets, sugar, stamps, confetti, paraffin, hatchets, whistles.

Dylan Thomas

1. Why does the poet describe the cobbles as 'sunhoneyed'?
   Make up ten combination words using two nouns in each case e.g. 'mudheaded'.
2. 'The gulls' gab and rabble' describes seagull sounds. Make up similar descriptions for
   (a) rooks; (b) turkeys; (c) budgies.
3. Describe morning in your home in short sentences. Begin like this, 'Dad is shaving, Mum complaining...'
4. Read the last two lines of the poem. Make a similar list for:
   (a) the contents of your schoolbag;
   (b) the contents of your garden shed/garage.
   (c) your favourite foods and sweets;
   (d) any flowers, trees and plants that come to mind.

1. This is a poem about words and the sounds of words. Organize a recital of the poem in the classroom to discover the 'Voice of Morningtown'.
2. Tape the poem and use sound-effects. Several people could recite different parts and in a variety of voices and accents.
3. 'Under Milk Wood' by Dylan Thomas is available on record. It is a play for voices and many sections make entertaining listening.

OGDEN NASH'S ZOO

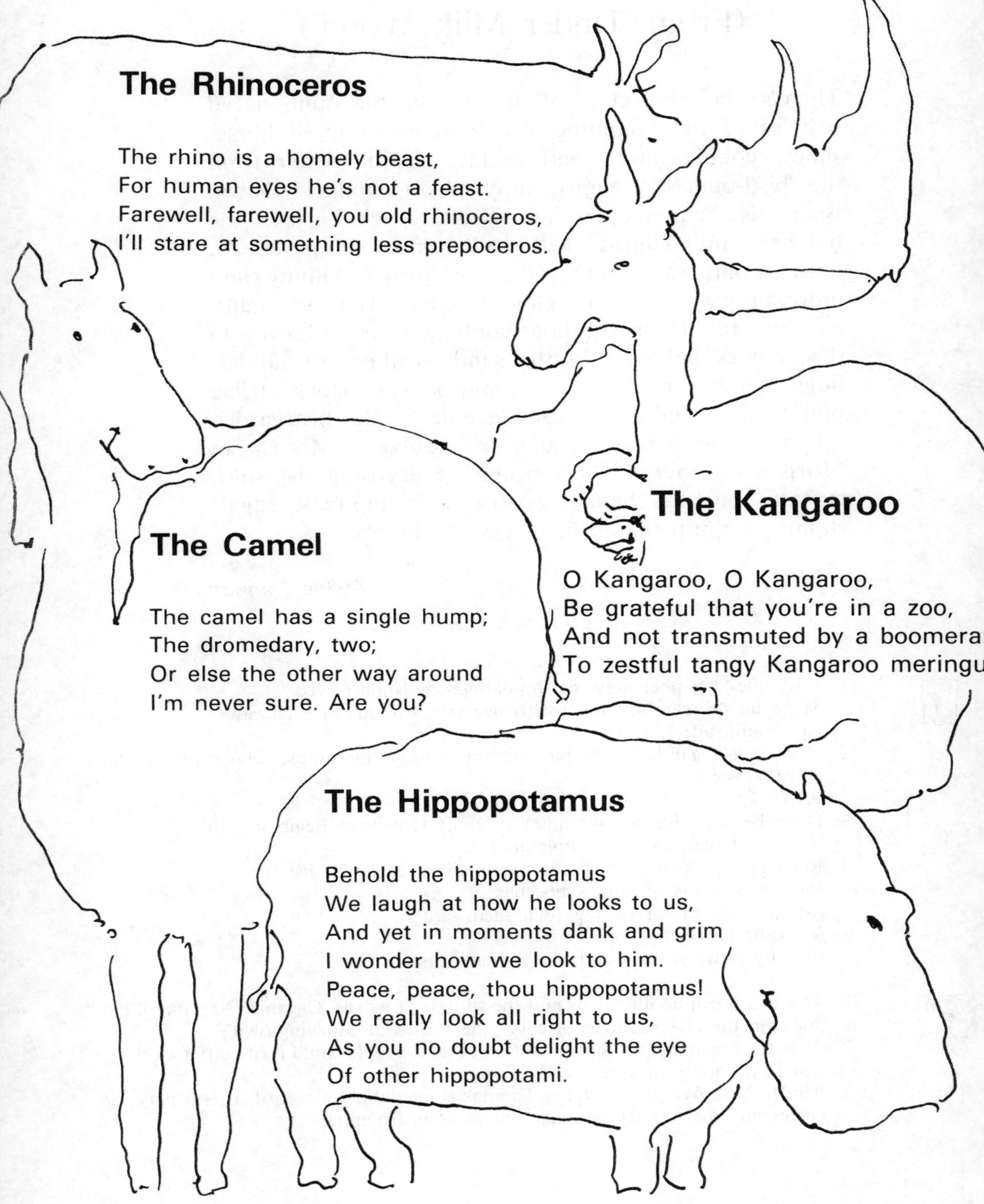

The Rhinoceros

The rhino is a homely beast,
For human eyes he's not a feast.
Farewell, farewell, you old rhinoceros,
I'll stare at something less prepoceros.

The Kangaroo

O Kangaroo, O Kangaroo,
Be grateful that you're in a zoo,
And not transmuted by a boomerar
To zestful tangy Kangaroo meringu

The Camel

The camel has a single hump;
The dromedary, two;
Or else the other way around
I'm never sure. Are you?

The Hippopotamus

Behold the hippopotamus
We laugh at how he looks to us,
And yet in moments dank and grim
I wonder how we look to him.
Peace, peace, thou hippopotamus!
We really look all right to us,
As you no doubt delight the eye
Of other hippopotami.

Now write your own short poems about the following animals:
a snake, an ostrich, a lioness, and a porcupine.

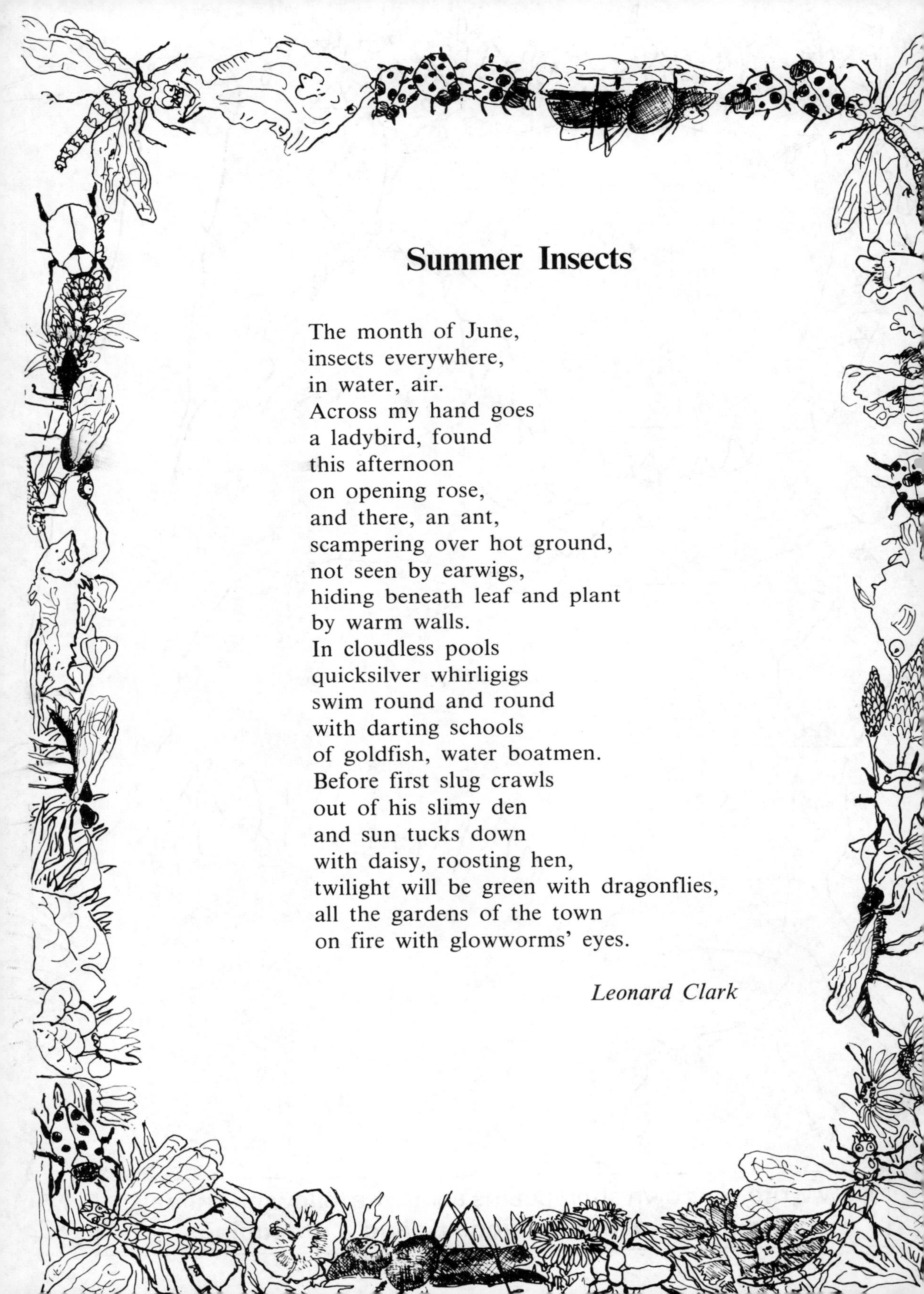

Summer Insects

The month of June,
insects everywhere,
in water, air.
Across my hand goes
a ladybird, found
this afternoon
on opening rose,
and there, an ant,
scampering over hot ground,
not seen by earwigs,
hiding beneath leaf and plant
by warm walls.
In cloudless pools
quicksilver whirligigs
swim round and round
with darting schools
of goldfish, water boatmen.
Before first slug crawls
out of his slimy den
and sun tucks down
with daisy, roosting hen,
twilight will be green with dragonflies,
all the gardens of the town
on fire with glowworms' eyes.

Leonard Clark

1. Make a list of the insects mentioned in the poem.
2. Name the insects in the poem that:
   (a) scamper; (b) swim round and round; (c) dart; (d) crawl.
3. Which of the creatures mentioned lives in water or on it?
4. A group of fish is called a school. Find collective nouns to describe groups of the following: —
   (a) starlings; (b) partridges; (c) bees; (d) lions; (e) dolphins; (f) wolves; (g) elephants.
5. Where do slugs hide, do you think?
6. Make a list of all the insects that visit your garden in summer.
7. Write a short description of twilight in the poet's garden.

1. Write a poem about summer in your garden. Begin with —
   'Summer in our garden.
   Everyone peeled, red, dead
   Casualties of the sun...
2. Write a short description of your garden:
   (a) in the morning; (b) in the evening; (c) at night.
   Model your sentences on the last 3 lines of the poem.

1. Make insect-masks during art class and organize an 'Insects' Ball' in the classroom. Everybody can take part.
   You could play such musical pieces as Waltz of the Flowers (Nutcracker Suite: Tchaikovsky), Pizzicato Polka (Strauss).
2. Organize a class project on insects.

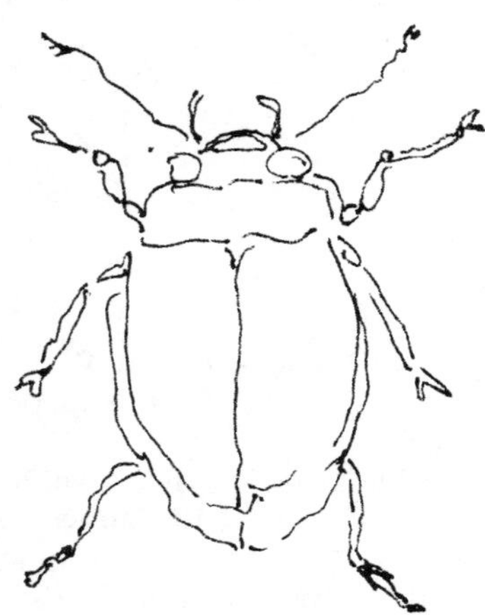

The Sea

The sea is a hungry dog.
Giant and grey.
He rolls on the beach all day.
With his clashing teeth and shaggy jaws
Hour upon hour he gnaws
The rumbling, tumbling stones,
And "Bones, bones, bones, bones!"
The giant sea-dog moans,
Licking his greasy paws.

And when the night wind roars
And the moon rocks in the stormy cloud,
He bounds to his feet and snuffs and sniffs,
Shaking his wet sides over the cliffs,
And howls and hollos long and loud.

But on quiet days in May or June,
When even the grasses on the dune
Play no more their reedy tune,
With his head between his paws
He lies on the sandy shores,
So quiet, so quiet, he scarcely snores

James Reeves

1. What colour is the sea on a stormy day?
2. Find three words to describe the sounds made by a wave when it breaks on the beach.
3. How does the poem describe the sea breaking over the cliffs?
4. What kind of tune is played by the dune grasses?
5. Which words best describe the sea on a quiet June day?: (a) tranquil; (b) restless; (c) untroubled; (d) edgy.

1. 'With his clashing teeth and shaggy jaws' is a description of a dog. Write similar descriptions of the following:
   (a) a cat drinking milk;
   (b) a cow munching grass;
   (c) a boy kicking a football;
   (d) a man chopping wood.

2. 'Rumbling, tumbling stones' is a description of the sounds made by stones when a wave retreats down a rocky beach.
   Write similar descriptions of the following:
   (a) trees in a storm;
   (b) a loud handclap;
   (c) footsteps on a wooden floor;
   (e) car tyres on a wet road;

Helicopter

Heli, Heli, Heli,
Copter,
Miss Brown was strolling when it stopped her;
Very, very nearly dropped her
Shopping-bag in sudden fright
At the monstrous clatter-flight.
All the men lean on their spades
And watch the flashing rotor-blades.
Gavin (watching television plays)
Yelled, 'Look, a coastal rescue chopper —
Most exciting thing for days —
Isn't it a yellow whopper?'
Like a maddened bumble-bee
It has him twisting round to see;
Makes all the village heads corkscrew
To wave a welcome to the crew,
Who nonchalant through open door
Wave as they squat upon the floor.
Gavin (and all the racing boys)
Rejoices in the noose of noise;
But stern Miss Brown now flushed with rage
Is scribbling a double page.
'Write to the paper, yes, I must;
I shall express my deep disgust.'
While in a near-by field the sheep,
A woolly, lumpy, startled heap.
Bolted,
Halted,
Cropped a
Little fainter
Bewildered by the helicopter.

Gregory Harrison

The Yellow Cat

'There he is,' yells Father,
Grabbing lumps of soil,
'That yellow tabby's on the fence.
Drown him in boiling oil.
He's scratching at my runner beans.
Bang at the window, quick.
Wait till I get my laces done
I'll beat him with my stick.'

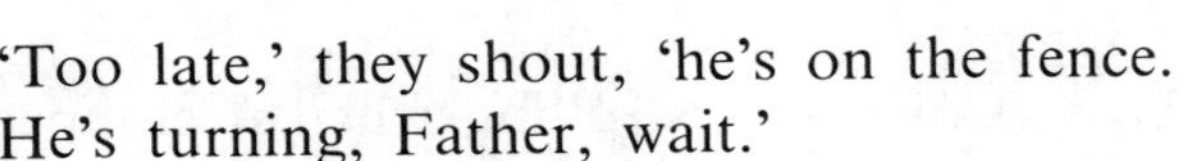

'Too late,' they shout, 'he's on the fence.
He's turning, Father, wait.'

'I'll give him turning, I'll be there,
I'll serve him on a plate.'

They banged the window, Father stormed
And hopped with wild despair;
The cat grew fat with insolence
And froze into a stare.
Its brazen glare stopped Father
With its blazing yellow light;
The silken shape turned slowly
And dropped gently out of sight.

Gregory Harrison

1. Where was everyone when Father spotted the yellow cat?
2. Why was Father so angry?
3. Did the children side with Father or with the yellow cat?
4. Draw a sketch of the cat on the wall. Write the cat's reply to Father in a speech-bubble.
5. Which words best describe the cat?:
   (a) dim-witted; (b) graceful; (c) haughty; (d) savage.
6. Which words best describe Father?:
   (a) outraged; (b) indignant; (c) murderous; (d) upset.

1. You are the yellow cat and you feel insulted. That night in the moonlight you change into a Pink Panther and return for your revenge.
   Tell the story.
2. The yellow cat is a poet. On the morning after the incident Father gets a poem in the post. It begins:
   'Some night when you are fast asleep
   I'll bring my catty friends...'
   Finish the poem.
3. Make a list of threats. e.g. 'I'll turn you into a legless centipede!'

1. Organize a project on cats. You will be surprised how many varieties there are.
2. The class can divide into groups. Each group will do a large collage of a Demon Cat. Assemble the Demon Cats in a wall frieze entitled 'Father's Nightmare'.
3. Listen to the 'Pink Panther Theme' composed by Henry Mancini.

Sneaky Bill

I'm Sneaky Bill, I'm terrible mean and vicious,
I steal all the cashews
from the mixed-nuts dishes;
I eat all the icing but I won't touch the cake,
And what you won't give me,
I'll go ahead and take.

I gobble the cherries from everyone's drinks,
And whenever there are sausages
I grab a dozen links;
I take both drumsticks if
there's turkey or chicken,
And the biggest strawberries
are what I'm pickin';

I make sure I get the finest chop on the plate,
And I'll eat the portions of anyone who's late!

I'm always on the spot before the dinner bell —
I guess I'm pretty awful,
But
I
do
eat
well!

William Cole

Colonel Fazackerley

Colonel Fazackerley Butterworth-Toast
Bought an old castle complete with a ghost,
But someone or other forgot to declare
To Colonel Fazack that the spectre was there.

On the very first evening, while waiting to dine,
The Colonel was taking a fine sherry wine,
When the ghost, with a furious flash and a flare,
Shot out of the chimney and shivered. 'Beware!'

Colonel Fazackerley put down his glass
And said, 'My dear fellow, that's really first class!
I just can't conceive how you do it at all.
I imagine you're going to a Fancy Dress Ball?'

At this, the dread ghost gave a withering cry.
Said the Colonel (his monocle firm in his eye),
'Now just how you do it I wish I could think.
Do sit down and tell me, and please have a drink.'

The ghost in his phosphorous cloak gave a roar
And floated about between ceiling and floor.
He walked through a wall and returned through a pane
And backed up the chimney and came down again.

Said the Colonel, 'With laughter I'm feeling quite weak!'
(As trickles of merriment ran down his cheek).
'My house-warming party I hope you won't spurn.
You *must* say you'll come and you'll give us a turn!'

At this, the poor spectre — quite out of his wits —
Proceeded to shake himself almost to bits.
He rattled his chains and he clattered his bones
And he filled the whole castle with mumbles and moans.

But Colonel Fazackerley, just as before,
Was simply delighted and called out, 'Encore!'
At which the ghost vanished, his efforts in vain,
And never was seen at the castle again.

'Oh dear, what a pity!' said Colonel Fazack.
'I don't know his name, so I can't call him back.'
And then with a smile that was hard to define,
Colonel Fazackerley went in to dine.

Charles Causley

Egg Thoughts

Soft Boiled
I do not like the way you slide,
I do not like your soft inside,
I do not like your many ways,
And I could do for many days
Without a soft-boiled egg.

Sunny-Side-Up
With their yolks and whites all runny
They are looking at me funny.

Sunny-Side-Down
Lying face-down on the plate
On their stomachs there they wait.

Poached
Poached eggs on toast, why do you shiver
With such a funny little quiver?

Scrambled
I eat as well as I am able,
But some falls underneath the table.

Hard-Boiled
With so much suffering today
Why do them any other way?

Russell Hoban

The *Alice Jean*

One moonlight night a ship drove in,
  A ghost ship from the west,
Drifting with bare mast and lone tiller;
  Like a mermaid drest
In long green weed and barnacles
  She beached and came to rest.

All the watchers of the coast
  Flocked to view the sight;
Men and women, streaming down
  Through the summer night,
Found her standing tall and ragged
  Beached in the moonlight.

Then one old woman stared aghast:
  'The *Alice Jean*? But no!
The ship that took my Ned from me
  Sixty years ago —
Drifted back from the utmost west
  With the ocean's flow?

'Caught and caged in the weedy pool
  Beyond the western brink,
Where crewless vessels lie and rot
  In waters black as ink,
Torn out at last by a sudden gale —
  Is it the *Jean*, you think?'

A hundred women gaped at her,
  The menfolk nudged and laughed,
But none could find a likelier story
  For the strange craft
With fear and death and desolation
  Rigged fore and aft.

The blind ship came forgotten home
  To all but one of these,
Of whom none dared to climb aboard her:
  And by and by the breeze
Veered hard about, and the *Alice Jean*
  Foundered in foaming seas.

Robert Graves

1. Can you explain why the *Alice Jean* sailed in by moonlight?
2. How does a tiller work? What does 'lone tiller' mean?
3. Do you believe that the *Alice Jean* simply drifted back to port? Can you put forward any other explanation?
4. Why did Ned leave his wife and go off to sea?
5. Do you think the crew of the *Alice Jean* were guilty of some terrible crime?
6. Which words best describe the feelings of the people watching: (a) relaxed; (b) fearful; (c) astonished; (d) uneasy; (e) amused?
7. Why did Ned's wife not go aboard the *Alice Jean*?
8. Find words similar in meaning to 'beached', 'ragged', 'brink', 'desolation', 'veered', 'foundered'.

1. You are the old woman. You decide to go on board the *Alice Jean*. Tell what happens. Begin like this:
   'On the deck I could see a shadow. His shadow? I could not believe it. And who had lowered the gangplank?. . . '
2. Draw a picture of a sailing ship and show the following, using your dictionary: stern, bow, prow, starboard, rudder, mainsail, crow's-nest.
3. Make up your own names for ships.

1. Make a wall picture of the *Alice Jean* in the weedy pool at the bottom of the sea. Glue on an assortment of objects such as strips of coloured crepe, raffia, etc. to represent seaweed and undersea creatures.
2. Organize a project on old sailing ships. Your school library and your local library should provide plenty of source material.
3. Play 'The Shipwreck' from 'Scheherezade' by Rimsky-Korsakov.

The Meadow Mouse

I

In a shoe box stuffed in an old nylon stocking
Sleeps the baby mouse I found in the meadow,
Where he trembled and shook beneath a stick
Till I caught him up by the tail and brought him in,
Cradled in my hand,
A little quaker, the whole body of him trembling,
His absurd whiskers sticking out like a cartoon-mouse,
His feet like small leaves,
Little lizard-feet,
Whitish and spread wide when he tried to struggle away,
Wriggling like a miniscule puppy.

Now he's eaten his three kinds of cheese and drunk from his
    bottle-cap watering-trough —
So much he just lies in one corner,
His tail curled under him, his belly big
As his head, his bat-like ears
Twitching, tilting toward the least sound.

Do I imagine he no longer trembles
When I come close to him?
He seems no longer to tremble.

II

But this morning the shoe-box house on the back porch is
empty.
Where has he gone, my meadow mouse,
My thumb of a child that nuzzled in my palm? —

To run under the hawk's wing,
Under the eye of the great owl watching from the elm-tree,
To live by courtesy of the shrike, the snake, the tom-cat.

I think of the nestling fallen into the deep grass,
The turtle gasping in the dusty rubble of the highway,
The paralytic stunned in the tub, and the water rising, —
All things innocent, hapless, forsaken.

Theodore Roethke

1. What kind of person is the poet?
2. How did he carry the baby mouse home?
3. Describe a cartoon-mouse.
4. Why does he describe the mouse as having 'little lizard-feet'?
5. Was the mouse happy in his new home?
6. Why does the poet describe the mouse as 'my thumb of a child'?
7. How does he feel when the mouse escapes? Do you think he was fond of the mouse?
8. What does 'hapless' mean?
9. What will happen to the fallen nestling, the turtle, and the paralytic mentioned at the end of the poem?
10. What will happen to the baby mouse, do you think?

1. Write a short poem describing a cat. Begin with —
   'Her paws like . . .
2. Imagine you are the baby mouse. Tell the story from your point of view.

1. Consult some nature books in your school library and find out what you can about the field-mouse.
2. 'The Mouse and his Child' by Russell Hoban and 'Mrs. Frisby and the Rats of Nimh' by Robert C. O'Brien are both marvellous books about mouse-characters. They make exciting reading.

The Starfish

Lord,
Your deep has closed over me.
Am I
some small Lucifer
fallen from heaven
and left
to be tormented by the waves?
Look, Lord,
I seem
a star of blood.
I try to remember
my lost royalty
but in vain.
Creeping over the sand,
I spread my star-points wide
and dream, dream, dream...
Lord,
an angel
could root me up
from the bottom of the sea
and set me back
in Your sky.
Oh! One day
could that be?

Amen.

Carmen Bernos De Gasztold

1. Explain 'Your deep has closed over me'.
2. What happened to Lucifer? How can the starfish be compared to Lucifer?
3. What sufferings must the starfish endure?
4. How does the starfish describe itself?
5. What request does the starfish ask of God?
6. What crime might the starfish be guilty of, in your opinion?
7. Complete this sentence. 'The bottom of the sea is the starfish's (....)?

1. You are a garden snail, You are convinced that once upon a time you were a showjumper. You resent this. Compose a prayer asking God to solve your problem. Begin like this:
   'Lord,
   A joke is a joke,
   But this hard saddle...'
2. You are a centipede with a family of nineteen. Write a letter to the Government complaining about the price of shoes.

1. Paint a picture of the sky at night — only your sky is full of starfish of many colours.
2. Paint a picture of the sea-bottom. Paint the moon and the planets swimming about with fins and gills. Do not include any starfish in your painting.

'Running Lightly Over Spongy Ground'

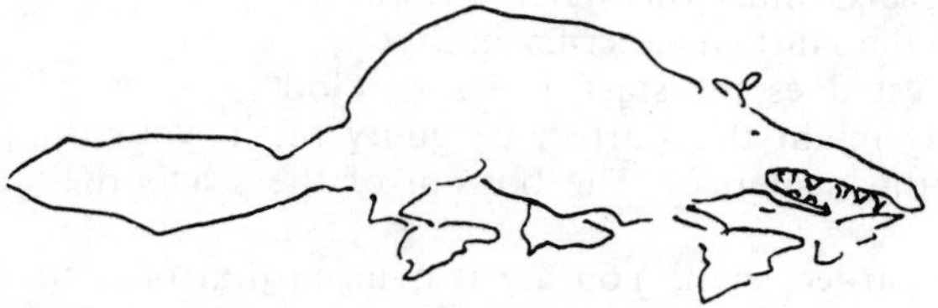

Running lightly over spongy ground,
Past the pasture of flat stones,
The three elms,
The sheep strewn on a field,
Over a rickety bridge
Toward the quick-water, wrinkling and rippling,

Hunting along the river,
Down among the rubbish, the bug-riddled foliage,
By the muddy pond-edge, by the bog-holes,
By the shrunken lake, hunting, in the heat of summer.

The shape of a rat?
It's bigger than that.
It's less than a leg
And more than a nose,
Just under the water
It usually goes.

Is it soft like a mouse?
Can it wrinkle its nose?
Could it come in the house
On the tips of its toes?

Take the skin of a cat
And the back of an eel,
Then roll them in grease, —
That's the way it would feel.

It's sleek as an otter
With wide webby toes
Just under the water
It usually goes.

Theodore Roethke

1. Is this creature fast or slow?
2. List all the objects and places it passes.
3. How do you know this creature is not afraid of being seen?
4. What is the creature fond of?
5. Who is asking the questions and who is answering them, do you think?
6. Suppose this creature were your pet and you had lost it.
   Send a description to the newspaper, offering a reward.
7. Have you identified the creature? Draw up a list of possible names for it?

1. Describe the following in the way the creature is described in verse 5:
   (a) a cat; (b) a hedgehog; (c) a worm; (d) your toes; (e) a sore throat.
2. 'Sleek as a otter' is a simile.
   Make up your own similes using the following words:
   (a) Big as...; (b) light as...; (c) dark as...; (d) hard as...

1. Paint a zoo of unusual animals. Each person in the class may paint his/her own animal. Arrange the pictures around the classroom but instead of a name each creature will have a description as in verses 5 and 6.

John Barleycorn

There were three men came out of the west
Their fortunes for to try,
And these three men made a solemn vow
John Barleycorn should die.

They've ploughed, they've sown, they've harrowed him in,
Throw'd clods upon his head,
And these three men made a solemn vow
John Barleycorn was dead.

They've let him lie for a very long time
Till the rain from heaven did fall,
Then little Sir John sprung up his head
And soon amazed them all.

They've let him stand till Midsummer Day
Till he looked both pale and wan,
And little Sir John's grown a long, long beard
And so become a man.

They've hired men with their scythes so sharp
To cut him off at the knee,
They've rolled and tied him by the waist,
Serving him most barb'rously.

They've hired men with their sharp pitch forks
Who pricked him to the heart,
And the loader he served him worse than that
For he's bound him to the cart.

They've wheeled him round and around the field
Till they came unto the barn
And there they've made a solemn mow
Of poor John Barleycorn.

They've hired men with the crabtree sticks
To cut him skin from bone,
And the miller he has served him worse than that
For he's ground him between two stones.

Here's little Sir John in the nut brown bowl
And here's brandy in the glass,
And little Sir John in the nut brown bowl
Proved the strongest man at last

For the huntsman he can't hunt the fox
And so loudly blow his horn
And the tinker he can't mend kettles nor pots
Without a little barleycorn.

Robert Burns

1. Were the three men murderers, in your opinion?
2. What tortures did John Barleycorn endure before the three men buried him?
3. How can you explain John Barleycorn's recovery?
4. Describe the tortures John Barleycorn was forced to suffer after Midsummer Day.
5. What, in simple language, is the liquid in the nut brown bowl?
6. Who is John Barleycorn?
7. Which words best describe this ballad?: (a) violent; (b) witty; (c) cruel; (d) cunning.

1. Make a similar ballad about milk/orange juice/potato crisps
2. You are the Lord Chief Justice of the Kitchen, and you never show mercy. You have found the following guilty of unmentionable crimes — a loaf of bread, a ripe banana, a packet of soap and a small pork chop. Read out the sentence on each:
   e.g. "Loaf of bread, you are condemned to be taken from the bread-bin and brought to the breadboard where first your heels will etc..."

1. Make a list of all the varieties of bread you know. Find a recipe for brown bread and write it into your copy.
2. Find out how many brands of whiskey are distilled in Ireland, and where the distilleries are located. In your 'John Barleycorn Corner' you can list the Irish brands in one column and the Scotch brands in another.

The Ballad of Kon-Tiki

ACROSS THE PACIFIC

They were not lonely. They found the sea
No barren waste but a living world,
Peopled as the woodland with wild creatures,
Curious and shy. The rough-riding steamer
With his foaming prow and his engine roar
Sees them not. But Kon-Tiki scared them not away.
As timid birds at twilight hop and twitter
On the summer lawn about the quiet house,
So now about the noiseless floating raft
The frolicking sea-dwellers. Then did Ocean,
The great showman, out of the bountiful deep
Conjure all manner of strange creatures
To delight them: flying fish that shot through the air
Like quicksilver, smack against the sail,
Then dropped to deck into the breakfast saucepan
Waiting there; the prosperous tunny,
Fat as an alderman with rows of double chins;
The glorious dolphin, bluebottle-green
With glittering golden fins, greedy
For the succulent weed that trailed like garlands
From the steering oar. There were many more —
Take the blue shark, a glutton
For blood; he'd swallow a dolphin, bones and all,
And crunch them like a concrete-mixer. They learnt
How to fool him with tit-bits, to get him
By his tail and haul aboard, skipping
Quickly from the snapping jaw —
He'd make a meal of anyone who let him!
(Rare sport this for the parrot who
For safety flew to the roof of the raft
And shrieked at the fun of it and laughed and laughed.)
Every kind they saw, from the million pilot fish
Tiny as a finger nail
To the majestic tremendous spotted whale,
Long as a tennis-court, who could —
Were he so minded — with one flick of his great tail
Have swatted them flat as a fly. But he couldn't be bothered.

Instead, circling cumbrously below,
He scratched his lazy back on the steering oar,
Till Erik sent him packing
With half a foot of steel in his spine.
Deep down he plunged, and the harpoon line —
Whipping through their hands — snapped like twine.

These marvels were the day's. What words
Can paint the night,
When the sea was no darkness but a universe of light?
Lo, in their wake a shoal
Of little shrimps, all shining,
A sprinkle of red coal!
Drawn by the gleaming cabin lamp, the octopus,
The giant squid with green ghostly eyes,
Hugged and hypnotized;
While, fathoms below, in the pitch-black deep were gliding

Balloons of flashing fire, silver
Streaming meteors. O world of wonder!
O splendid pageantry!
Hour after dreamy hour they gazed spell-bound,
Trailing their fingers in the starry sea.

Ian Serraillier

1. What advantage had the raft over ships with engines?
2. Why is the ocean compared to a showman?
3. Make two columns. In one column list all the sea-creatures mentioned in the poem. In the other make a list of all the colours mentioned. Join each creature to its colour.
4. Which is your favourite creature and why?
5. Name the largest and the smallest creature mentioned in the poem.
6. Why is a pilot-fish so called?
7. Do you think Erik was right to harpoon the spotted whale?

1. Take each creature mentioned and compare it to something else. e.g. 'the majestic spotted whale as long as a tennis court' '.
2. You are the whale Erik has harpooned. You are very angry. Tell what happens.

1. Divide the class into groups. Each group will paint a scene taken from the poem e.g. the night scene. Link all the paintings in a frieze around the classroom wall.
2. Organize a discussion on whale-hunting, seal-pup clubbing and matters of maritime conservation. etc.
3. Listen to Elgar's 'Sea Symphony'

Night Mail
(From the G.P.O. film)

This is the night mail crossing the border,
Bringing the cheque and the postal order,
Letters for the rich, letters for the poor,
The shop at the corner and the girl next door.
Pulling up Beattock, a steady climb —
The gradient's against her, but she's on time.

Past cotton grass and moorland boulder
Shovelling white steam over her shoulder,
Snorting noisily as she passes
Silent miles of wind-bent grasses.

Birds turn their heads as she approaches,
Stare from the bushes at her black-faced coaches.
Sheep dogs cannot turn her course,
They slumber on with paws across.
In the farm she passes no one wakes,
But a jug in the bedroom gently shakes.

Dawn freshens, the climb is done.
Down towards Glasgow she descends
Towards the steam tugs yelping down the glade of cranes,
Towards the fields of apparatus, the furnaces
Set on the dark plain like gigantic chessman.
All Scotland waits for her:
In the dark glens, beside the pale-green lochs
Men long for news.

Letters of thanks, letters from banks,
Letters of joy from girl and boy,
Receipted bills and invitations
To inspect new stock or visit relations,
And applications for situations
And timid lovers' declarations

And gossip, gossip, from all the nations,
News circumstantial, news financial,
Letters with holiday snaps to enlarge in,
Letters with faces scrawled in the margin,
Letters from uncles, cousins and aunts,
Letters to Scotland from the South of France,
Letters of condolence to Highlands and Lowlands,
Notes from overseas to Hebrides —
Written on paper of every hue,
The pink, the violet, the white and the blue,
The chatty, the catty, the boring, adoring,
The cold and official and the heart's outpouring
Clever, stupid, short and long,
The typed and the printed and the spelt all wrong.

Thousands are still asleep
Dreaming of terrifying monsters,
Or a friendly tea beside the band at Cranston's or Crawford's
Asleep in working Glasgow, asleep in well-set
Edinburgh,
Asleep in granite Aberdeen,
They continue their dreams;
But shall wake soon and long for letters,
And none will hear the postman's knock
Without a quickening of the heart,
For who can hear and feel himself forgotten?

W. H. Auden

1. Name some of the things the train passes on its way to Glasgow?
2. Write your own description of the train travelling.
3. Write your own description of the train descending to Glasgow.
4. At what time of day does the train reach Glasgow?
5. Make a list of five of the most important letters the train is carrying.
6. What lines tell you that the train is slowing down?

The class may recite this poem together. Changes of tone will add to the general impression of a train travelling

The Diver

I put on my aqua-lung and plunge
Exploring, like a ship with a glass keel,
The secrets of the deep. Along my lazy road
On and on I steal —
Over waving bushes which at a touch explode
Into shrimps, then closing, rock to the tune of the tide;
Over crabs that vanish in puffs of sand,
Look, a string of pearls bubbling at my side
Breaks in my hand —
Those pearls were my breath!... Does that hollow hide
Some old Armada wreck in seaweed furled,
Crusted with barnacles, her cannon rusted,
The great *San Philip?* What bullion in her hold?
Pieces of eight, silver crowns, and bars of solid gold?

I shall never know. Too soon the clasping cold
Fastens on flesh and limb
And pulls me to the surface. Shivering, back I swim
To the beach, the noisy crowds, the ordinary world.

Ian Serraillier

1. Where is a ship's keel located? How can the diver be compared to a ship with a glass keel?
2. Imagine you are the diver. Describe the sounds you hear as you breathe.
3. What was the Armada? What happened to it? What does San Philip mean?
4. Do you think the diver has discovered a treasure-ship?
5. Write a description of a crab walking. Begin like this:
   'Like a house on stilts the crab...'
6. Why did the diver have to surface?

1. 'Along my lazy road on and on I steal...' is how the diver describes his movement. Make up similar sentences to describe each of the following:
   (a) a bird flying;
   (b) a tortoise walking;
   (c) an athlete sprinting.
2. List and describe occasions on which you have had the experience of sudden change e.g. coming out of a cinema.

1 Make a colourful wall-frieze based on the poem.
2. Collect any treasure stories you can find from newspapers, magazines, books, comics, etc. Arrange a 'Treasure Corner' in the classroom. You may also display any foreign coins or objects of interest you have collected.

Digging for China

'Far enough down is China,' somebody said.
'Dig deep enough and you might see the sky
As clear as the bottom of a well.
Except it would be real — a different sky.
Then you could burrow down until you came
To China! Oh, it's nothing like New Jersey.
There's people, trees, and houses, and all that,
But much, much different. Nothing looks the same.'

I went and got the trowel out of the shed
And sweated like a coolie all that morning,
Digging a hole beside the lilac-bush,
Down on my hands and knees. It was a sort
Of praying, I suspect. I watched my hand
Dig deep and darker, and I tried and tried
To dream a place where nothing was the same.
The trowel never did break through to blue.

Before the dream could weary of itself
My eyes were tired of looking into darkness,
My sunbaked head of hanging down a hole.
I stood up in a place I had forgotten,
Blinking and staggering while the earth went round
And showed me silver barns, the fields dozing
In palls of brightness, patens growing and gone
In the tides of leaves, and the whole sky china blue.
Until I got my balance back again
All that I saw was China, China, China.

Richard Wilbur

Questions

1. How old is the boy in the poem?
2. What country is the poem set in?
3. Name some of the things the boy expected to see when he reached China?
4. What did he mean by 'It was a sort of praying, I suspect'?
5. Describe the boy's feelings when he stood up suddenly. What did he see?
6. Explain the following words: — coolie, pail, paten.

The Snare

I hear a sudden cry of pain!
There is a rabbit in a snare;
Now I hear the cry again,
But I cannot tell from where.

But I cannot tell from where
He is calling out for aid;
Crying on the frightened air,
Making everything afraid.

Making everything afraid,
Wrinkling up his little face,
As he cries again for aid;
And I cannot find the place!

And I cannot find the place
Where his paw is in the snare;
Little one! Oh, little one!
I am searching everywhere.

James Stephens

1. How would you describe the poet?:
   (a) alert; (b) sympathetic; (c) hungry; (d) concerned.
2. Describe a snare. How does a snare trap a rabbit?
3. Write a brief description of a rabbit.
4. What effect does the rabbit's cry have on other creatures?
5. Which words best describe the person's feelings in verse 4.?:
   (a) anxious; (b) fretful; (c) curious; (d) distraught.

1. Write a poem about a bird in a cage.
2. You are searching for the rabbit. Suddenly you are caught in a huge snare. A gigantic rabbit comes from behind a furze-bush. He is carrying a knife and fork. 'Ah, dinner', says the rabbit. Continue the story.

The Wayfarer

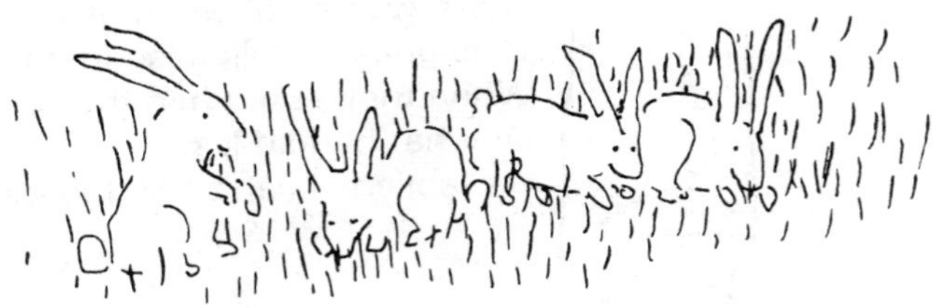

The beauty of the world hath made me sad,
This beauty that will pass;
Sometimes my heart hath shaken with great joy
To see a leaping squirrel in a tree,
Or a red lady-bird upon a stalk,
Or little rabbits in a field at evening,
Lit by a slanting sun,
Or some green hill where shadows drifted by,
Some quiet hill where mountainy man hath sown
And soon will reap, near to the gate of Heaven;
Or children with bare feet upon the sands
Of some ebbed sea, or playing on the streets
Of little towns in Connacht,
Things young and happy.
And then my heart hath told me:
These will pass,
Will pass and change, will die and be no more,
Things bright and green, things young and happy;
And I have gone upon my way
Sorrowful.

Padraic Pearse 1879-1916

Questions

1. How does the poet describe his happiness?
2. What things especially pleased him?
3. What time of year is described in the poem?
4. What part of Ireland is the poem describing?
5. What is the meaning of the phrase "near to the gate of Heaven"?
6. Why is the poet sad?
7. Explain why 'The Wayfarer' is a suitable title for the poem?

There was an old woman of Ryde.
Who ate some green apples and died.
Inside the lamented,
The apples fermented,
Making cider inside 'er inside.

There was an old man of Tarentum
Who gnashed his false teeth till he bent 'em.
When they asked him the cost
Of what he had lost,
He replied: 'I can't say: I just rent 'em.

The bottle of perfume that Willie sent
Was highly displeasing to Millicent.
Her thanks were so cold
That they quarrelled, I'm told,
Through that silly scent Willie sent Millicent.

There was a young bard of Japan
Whose limericks never would scan;
When they said it was so,
He replied, 'Yes I know,
But I make a rule of always trying to get just as many words into the last line as I possibly can.'

THE LIMERICK TRAIN

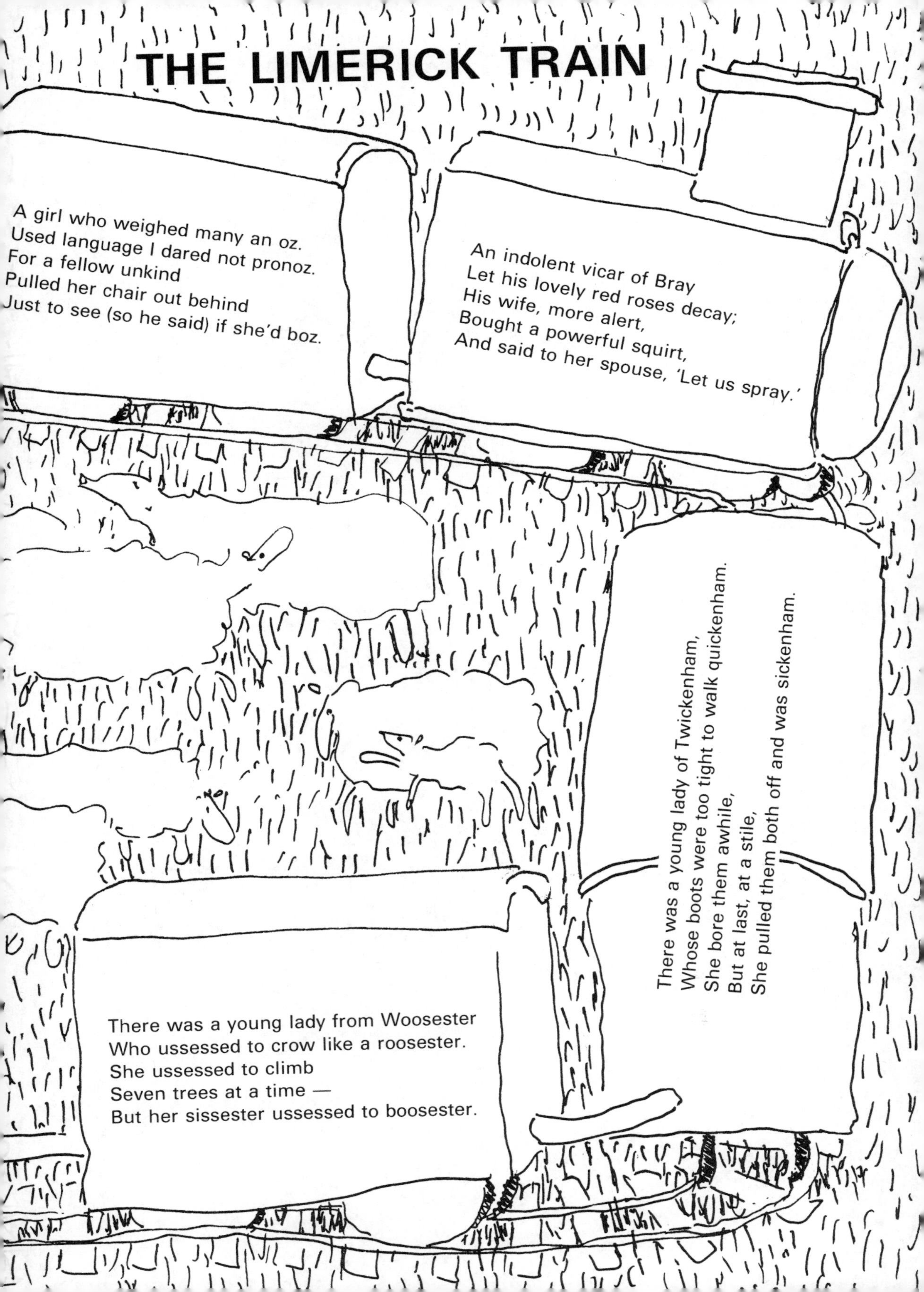

A girl who weighed many an oz.
Used language I dared not pronoz.
For a fellow unkind
Pulled her chair out behind
Just to see (so he said) if she'd boz.

An indolent vicar of Bray
Let his lovely red roses decay;
His wife, more alert,
Bought a powerful squirt,
And said to her spouse, 'Let us spray.'

There was a young lady of Twickenham,
Whose boots were too tight to walk quickenham.
She bore them awhile,
But at last, at a stile,
She pulled them both off and was sickenham.

There was a young lady from Woosester
Who ussessed to crow like a roosester.
She ussessed to climb
Seven trees at a time —
But her sissester ussessed to boosester.